BRITAIN'S SECOND-HAND

TRAMS

AN HISTORIC OVERVIEW

BRITAIN'S SECOND-HAND

TRAMS

AN HISTORIC OVERVIEW

PETER WALLER

PEN & SWORD
TRANSPORT

AN IMPRINT OF PEN & SWORD BOOKS LTD.
YORKSHIRE – PHILADELPHIA

Britain's Second-Hand Trams: An Historic Overview

First published in Great Britain in 2021 by
Pen and Sword Transport
An imprint of
Pen & Sword Books Ltd
Yorkshire - Philadelphia

ISBN 978 1 52673 897 4

Typeset in 11/13 Palatino by SJmagic DESIGN SERVICES, India.

Printed and bound in India by Replika Press Pvt. Ltd.

Pen & Sword Books Ltd incorporates the Imprints of Pen & Sword Books Archaeology, Atlas, Aviation,
Battleground, Discovery, Family History, History, Maritime, Military, Naval, Politics, Railways, Select,
Transport, True Crime, Fiction, Frontline Books, Leo Cooper, Praetorian Press, Seaforth Publishing,
Wharncliffe and White Owl.

For a complete list of Pen & Sword titles please contact

PEN & SWORD BOOKS LIMITED
47 Church Street, Barnsley, South Yorkshire, S70 2AS, England
E-mail: enquiries@pen-and-sword.co.uk
Website: www.pen-and-sword.co.uk

or

PEN AND SWORD BOOKS
1950 Lawrence Rd, Havertown, PA 19083, USA
E-mail: Uspen-and-sword@casematepublishers.com
Website: www.penandswordbooks.com

CONTENTS

ABBREVIATIONS

BEC	British Electric Car Co Ltd, Trafford Park, Manchester
BET	British Electric Traction
BTH	British Thomson-Houston Co Ltd
EMB	Electro-Mechanical Brake Co Ltd
ER&TCW	Electric Railway & Tramway Carriage Works Ltd
L&CBER	Llandudno & Colwyn Bay Electric Railway
LCCTT	London County Council Tramways Trust
LPTB	London Passenger Transport Board
LRTA	Light Rapid Transit Association
LRTL	Light Railway Transport League
LTE	London Transport Executive
LTHG	London Tramways History Group
LUT	London United Tramways
M&G	Mountain & Gibson
M&T	Maley & Taunton
MET	Metropolitan Electric Tramways
MTMS	Manchester Tramway/Transport Museum Society
PET	Potteries Electric Traction Co Ltd
SHMD	Stalybridge, Hyde, Mossley & Dukinfield Tramways & Electricity Board
SLT	South Lancashire Tramways
South Met	South Metropolitan Electric Tramways & Lighting Co Ltd
STMS/STTS	Scottish Tramway Museum Society/Scottish Tramway & Transport Society
TLRS	Tramway & Light Railway Society
UDC	Urban District Council
UEC	United Electric Car Co Ltd

ACKNOWLEDGEMENTS

The majority of the images in this book have been drawn from the collections held by the Online Transport Archive; these include the following: the late Geoffrey Ashwell, the late C. Carter, the late Ian L. Cormack, Barry Cross, the late D.W.K. Jones, the late R.W.A. Jones, the late J. Joyce, the late F.N.T. Lloyd-Jones, the late John McCann, the late John Meredith, the late Ronnie Stephens, the late Phil Tatt, the late Julian Thompson, the late F.E.J. Ward, the late Peter N. Williams and Ian L. Wright. The National Tramway Museum houses the negatives of the late W.A. Camwell, the late Maurice O'Connor, the late R.B. Parr and the late H.B. Priestley. As with my earlier books, I'd like to express my sincere thanks to Martin Jenkins for ideas and comments on the book.

INTRODUCTION

In the course of the history of Britain's first generation electric tramways, tens of thousands of new tramcars were acquired. The vast majority of these were to be operated for their entire working life – which may have been relatively short or decades long – by a single owner. However, almost from the start of electric era, a significant number of trams were to be purchased by or transferred to a second (or even, in a limited number of cases, a third) operator.

In the early years, the transfers were for practical reasons; trams were exchanged between subsidiaries of the same company – such as those that were exchanged between Coventry and Norwich (both subsidiaries of the New General Traction Co) – where traffic considerations necessitated. A number of systems acquired tramcars at opening that reflected the optimism of the promoters; sometimes this was misplaced with the result that trams with a large capacity were exchanged for or replaced by smaller vehicles more suited to the traffic levels generated. In a small number of cases, orders for one operator were rejected – possibly on grounds of quality – and re-sold to a second operator.

During both world wars, a number of systems required additional tramcars to increase capacity at a time when vast numbers were required to get to and from factories employed in the war effort. There was also the need – as in the case of Sheffield Corporation during the Second World War – to acquire replacement trams quickly to replace cars that had been damaged beyond repair as a result of enemy action.

The primary factor behind the transfer of trams from one operator to a second was the conversion of systems from tram to either bus or trolleybus operation where systems that had a longer-term future took advantage of trams withdrawn that still had some years of operational life left in them. A number of relatively early casualties acquired new trams towards the end of the system's life and these readily found a new home when the second-hand price was considerably lower than that of acquiring wholly new cars. A number of operators – most notably Leeds and Sunderland – took advantage of the conversion of systems such as London, Hull and Manchester to acquire relatively new tramcars. One system that sought to exploit the second-hand market in the early 1950s was Dundee; its ageing fleet of traditional four-wheel cars was rightly considered to be a liability. The corporation looked at the purchase of new trams, but this was deemed too expensive, and then considered the purchase of a number of second-hand cars. The sad fact was, however, that the separation between the running lines on much of the network was much narrower than usual; this precluded the purchase of virtually all available standard gauge trams and so the system was to survive through until October 1956 relying on trams, many of which had their origins in vehicles delivered some 50 years earlier.

The final second-hand trams were the streamlined bogie cars that were sold from Liverpool to Glasgow in the mid-1950s. These were destined to have a relatively short life north of the border as, by the time they entered service, Glasgow – one of the most secure of British tramways in the years immediately after the end of the Second World War – had introduced its own abandonment policy. This epitomises one of the sad facts about all of the trams featured in this book; their careers as second-hand cars was often very limited as the new owners succumbed to the fashion for conversion. In Leeds, some of the second-hand 'Feltham' cars acquired between 1949 and 1951 never actually entered service, being scrapped – still in their London Transport livery – in the mid-1950s having made the journey to the West Riding only to spend the next few years in storage. Some of those that did enter service lasted only a handful of years before they made their final trip to the scrapyard.

There are a couple of points that are worth considering. Firstly, there was not only a market for complete trams. There was also a considerable trade in spares and other parts, from motors to traction columns. For example, the L&CBER acquired a range of material from Birmingham Corporation following the latter's final abandonment in 1953 whilst Liverpool Corporation used second-hand traction columns on its extension to Kirby. There was also an export market for complete trams and equipment; for example, a number of Cardiff Corporation single-deck cars were sold to Brazil. Finally, there are a number of cases where operators either sought or were offered second-hand trams where, for a variety of reasons, a deal proved impossible. For example, with the abandonment of the Aberdeen system in 1958, the corporation tried to sell the twenty trams – Nos 19-38 – that were new in 1949 to Blackpool Corporation. Sadly this came to nothing and the trams were scrapped when less than a decade old.

This book is an exploration of these electric trams that ran in second-hand service. Excluded are the considerable number of trams that passed from one operator to a successor where that successor merely inherited the fleet from an earlier operator or lessor. Thus, the vast number of trams acquired by the LPTB in 1933 from the various councils and companies are not covered, for example, nor are the trams taken over by Bradford Corporation from the Mid-Yorkshire Tramways Co. What is portrayed are those trams that, for whatever reason, generally made a physical journey from one operator to a second, such as the ex-Hull, London, Manchester, Southampton and Sunderland trams that were to be operated by Leeds Corporation.

Ex-MET No 2105 is seen departing from Charlton Works for the final time following its withdrawal in September 1950 en route to its new life in the West Riding of Yorkshire. It would emerge as Leeds No 511 the following year and survive through until August 1957. The movement of second-hand trams was generally undertaken by road and, given the number of low railway bridges across the country, must have been carefully planned. Often – as in this case – the body and truck or bogies would have been separated, only to be reunited once received by the new operator. In the case of the 'Felthams' supplied to Leeds, the bogies sent north were generally not used under the same cars as they had been used with in London. *Barry Cross Collection/Online Transport Archive*

It's 6 June 1949 and one of the cars sold by Southampton Corporation to Leeds Corporation stands in Shirley depot yard prior to being loaded on to a lorry for its move northwards. The tram has been jacked up and its truck removed to facilitate its transfer. Note that all identification, including fleet name and number, has been removed. *Julian Thompson/Online Transport Archive*

Another second-hand acquisition by Leeds Corporation – this time ex-Manchester Corporation 'Pilcher' No 370 – is seen receiving attention in Kirkstall Road Works. This car had been withdrawn in Manchester during June 1948 and was to re-enter service in the West Riding on 1 January 1949 as Leeds No 286. Finally withdrawn on 3 April 1954 – one of the last two of the ex-Manchester cars to survive in Leeds – No 286 was scrapped at Low Field Road towards the end of the following month. *F.E.J. Ward/Online Transport Archive*

Above: **The purchase** and transport of the trams was but part of the process of acquiring second-hand cars; inevitably, given that the systems that they were purchased from were in decline, many of the trams required considerable work before they were ready to re-enter service. This view, taken in the Kirkstall Road Works of Leeds Corporation, shows work in progress on the refurbishment of three ex-Southampton trams following their arrival in the West Riding during the summer of 1949. The car on the left is ex-Southampton No 104 which became Leeds No 295; this entered service following overhaul and repainting on 4 February 1950. In the centre is ex-Southampton No 105 – note the chalked number plus that of its Leeds identity (No 294) on the outside of the exposed staircase; this re-entered service in November 1949. The third car is unidentified. Unfortunately, none of the eleven ex-Southampton cars that operated in Leeds was destined to survive long; all had been withdrawn and scrapped by the end of 1953. *F.E.J. Ward/Online Transport Archive*

Opposite above: **It was** not only entire trams that were disposed of following withdrawal; there was a ready market for equipment. Prior to the Second World War, a 3ft 6in gauge electric railway operated along Felixstowe Pier – one of the longest piers in country when it was completed in 1905 – and, following the demise of the 3ft 6in trams operated by Ipswich Corporation on 26 July 1926, the pier railway acquired some surplus equipment, including this four-wheel truck, for reuse. During the war, the pier was sectioned as a precaution to prevent being used in any German invasion and was partially demolished after the war. The pier railway was never reinstated and the truck and equipment are seen in derelict condition in this post-war view. *V.C. Jones*

Opposite below: **Over the** years, a significant number of tramway bodies found a second use as holiday homes or sheds; here, three ex-London Transport 'E/1' bodies have found a new home on Hayling Island. A number of today's preserved trams owe their survival to having spent many years in gardens and fields. *G.F. Ashwell/Online Transport Archive*

For a number of these cars, however, their second life was to be relatively short; here ex-London Transport 'E/1' No 931 is being broken up on Hayling Island on 14 September 1947. *G.F. Ashwell/Online Transport Archive*

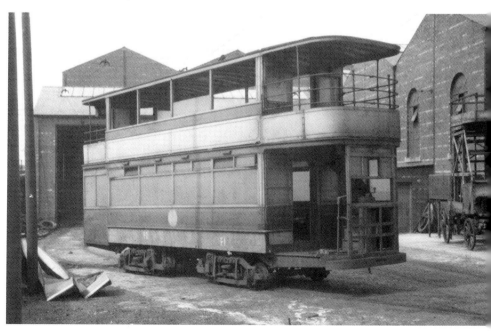

In 1932 South Shields Corporation acquired six trams from Wigan Corporation; two of these never re-entered service but four were rebuilt as fully enclosed, becoming South Shields Nos 23 (ii), 50-52. This view records one of the ex-South Shields cars; judging by its condition, this is probably one of two that were not rebuilt and which were scrapped in 1934. Note the horse-drawn tower wagon in the background. *John Nicol/National Tramway Museum*

SECOND-HAND TRAMS

The first electric tramway in London was the Alexandra Palace Electric Railway, which opened on 13 May 1898. The short – 600 yard – line was provided with four single-deck combination cars built by Waggonfabrik Falkenreid of Hamburg. The pioneering line was, however, short-lived and closed with Alexandra Palace at the end of the 1899 season on 30 September. The four cars were then sold in 1901 to the Great Grimsby Street Tramways Co, where three were rebuilt into open-top double-deck – Nos 25, 26 and 28 – and re-entered service during 1903 and 1904. This view records one of the quartet undergoing rebuilding work prior to re-entering service. In 1908, the original trucks, built by Falkenreid, were replaced by Brill 21E four-wheel trucks reused from Nos 5, 6, 10 and 19 that dated to 1900. Latterly Nos 26 and 28 were used as rail grinders. The quartet was withdrawn by 1929 when the fleet numbers were reused for some of the ex-Gosport & Fareham cars acquired that year. *Barry Cross Collection/Online Transport Archive*

Above: **Although three** of the ex-Alexandra Palace cars were rebuilt as open-top trams, the fourth – No 27 – was completed with a fully-enclosed top deck – the first tram in Britain to be so equipped. The top cover was designed and patented by H.L. White, who had been appointed manager of the Great Grimsby company in 1901, and the rebuilt car made its inaugural run on 1 August 1903. It was to survive in service until the arrival of the ex-Gosport & Fareham cars in 1930 and was scrapped thereafter. *H. Orme White/via D.W.K. Jones Collection/ Online Transport Archive*

Opposite above: **By the** end of 1900, the Swansea Improvements & Tramways Co Ltd was operating a fleet of forty-one trams. Thirty of these were single-deckers – Nos 1-30 – supplied by Brush; the remaining eleven – Nos 31-41 – are more of a mystery. These were also completed with Brush bodies but were fitted with Peckham 9A Cantilever trucks rather than the Baltimore four-wheel trucks on the original thirty. It seems probable that these cars represent eleven of the twelve cars supplied by BTH to Leeds Corporation as part of a batch of fifty open-top four-wheel cars – Nos 133-182 – delivered in 1899. Leeds rejected these twelve cars – Nos 143-54 – and returned them to the supplier. With replacement equipment, eleven were sold to Swansea where they initially operated as single-deck although were converted to open-top double-deck form by the end of 1900. It is in this guise that No 32 is pictured on Oxford Street, Swansea. The bulk of the Swansea fleet was single-deck as a result of a number of low railway bridges; as rebuilt as double-deck cars, the batch was limited to the St Helens route. *Barry Cross Collection/Online Transport Archive*

Opposite below: **The eleven** open-top double-deck cars – Nos 31-41 – operated by the Swansea Improvements & Tramways Co Ltd were all to be fitted with open-balcony top covers – either supplied by UEC or completed in the company's own workshops – during 1907 and 1908 and this view records No 36 with its new top cover passing the Exeter Hotel, in Oxford Street. *Barry Cross Collection/ Online Transport Archive*

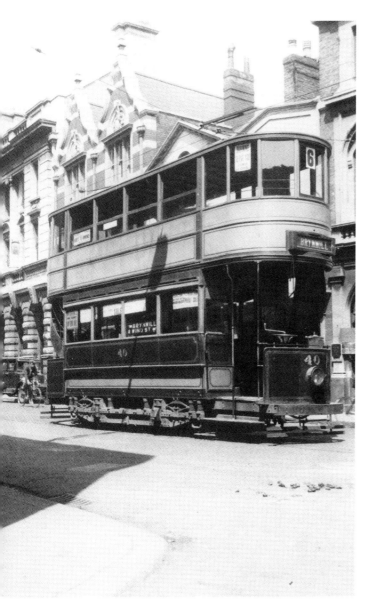

Above left: **One of** the Swansea Improvements & Tramways Co Ltd cars – No 34 – was subsequently rebuilt, in about 1919, with a fully-enclosed top deck and was subsequently renumbered 40; it is seen here after renumbering. The numbers of three of the ex-Leeds cars – Nos 31-33 - were reused by new fully-enclosed cars built in 1929 and two more – Nos 34 and 35 – followed in 1933 (construction of No 34 presumably resulting in the renumbering of the older car). The list of sixty-nine operational cars in the Swansea fleet in 1933 provided in the late Henry Priestley's article in *Tramway Review* on the history of the operator excludes all of the ex-Leeds cars and so the assumption must be that all had been withdrawn by that date. *Barry Cross Collection/Online Transport Archive*

Above right: **In 1899** Brush supplied a batch of five open-top cars – Nos 464-68 – to Liverpool Corporation; these were fitted with the Brush version of the Peckham Cantilever four-wheel truck and the supplier claimed that these were the first trams supplied in their entirety by a single manufacturer. Unfortunately, Liverpool declined to pay for them and so they were returned to Brush. However, in 1900, Leeds Corporation had an urgent need for additional trams and so agreed to purchase the quintet at £445 each. The cars – Nos 44, 46, 55, 79 and 83 – entered service in May 1900. Between July and October 1910 all were equipped with enclosed top covers of the 'glass-house'-type as evinced by No 44 pictured at Thwaite Gate, Hunslet, in about 1912. All five were to be retrucked in 1922 although No 83 was to be withdrawn later that year. The remaining four were all withdrawn during 1926 and 1927. *Barry Cross Collection/Online Transport Archive*

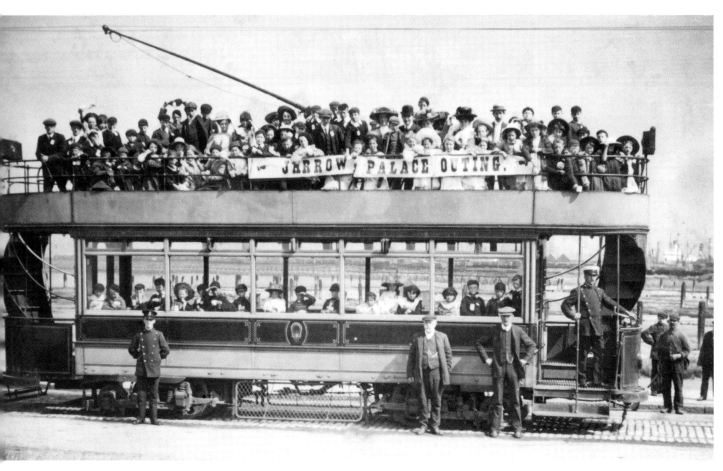

For the opening of the Gravesend & Northfleet Electric Tramways on 2 August 1902, ER&TCW supplied ten open-top trams fitted with Brill 22E bogies. However, the expected level of business of the new operator was not achieved and as a result, the company decided to dispose of the ten trams to other operators within the BET group. The first two – probably Nos 9 and 10 (as new demi cars with those numbers were ordered and delivered in early 1904) – were sold to Jarrow & District Electric Tramways Co Ltd where they became Nos 5 and 6. They remained in service until the conversion of the Jarrow system on 30 June 1929 and were then sold for further operation, this time to South Shields Corporation (see page 76). *Barry Cross Collection/Online Transport Archive*

During 1897 and 1898, the 3ft 6in gauge Coventry Electric Tramways Co Ltd – a subsidiary of the New General Traction Co Ltd – acquired a batch of ten uncanopied open-top trams from Brush; Nos 11-20 were equipped with Peckham 9A four-wheel cantilever trucks. Another subsidiary of the company – the Norwich Electric Tramways Co Ltd – operated forty very similar trams, Nos 1-40, and, in 1904, two of the Coventry cars – Nos 19 and 20 – were transferred to Norwich, becoming Nos 41 and 42 in the fleet. One of the two cars – No 20 – is seen in operation with Coventry in 1899. *Barry Cross Collection/Online Transport Archive*

Above: **Between 1923** and 1930, the Norwich Electric Tramways Co Ltd acquired thirty-four replacement bodies from English Electric and fitted them to the existing trucks (reused from the withdrawn cars). Amongst the trams so treated were Nos 41 and 42 – during 1924 and 1928 respectively – and here No 41 is seen in its rebuilt form outside the company's Silver Road depot alongside similarly reconstructed Nos 28 and 38. The final Norwich trams operated on 10 December 1935. *Hugh Nicol/National Tramway Museum*

Opposite: **In 1904,** the Oldham, Ashton & Hyde Electric Tramway Ltd exchanged eight single-deck trailer cars – Nos 27-34 – for four of the Middleton Electric Traction Co's single-deck combination cars that dated to 1902. ER&TCW constructed a batch of ten combination cars – Nos 11-20 – fitted with Brill 22E bogies for the opening of the Middleton company's operations. The cars that passed to the Oldham, Ashton & Hyde were four of Nos 11, 14, 16, 17 and 18; they were to become Oldham, Ashton & Hyde Nos 27-30. The remaining six Middleton cars were sold – without motors – to the Swansea Improvements & Tramways Co Ltd (see page 26), another subsidiary of BET. Following the transfer of the assets of the Oldham, Ashton & Hyde Electric Tramway Ltd to Ashton, Hyde and Manchester corporations on 1 July 1921, Hyde Corporation took possession of a number of ex-company cars – including two of the ex-Middleton cars (Nos 29/30) – and added them to the fleet of the Stalybridge, Hyde, Mossley & Dukinfield Transport & Electricity Board, where both retained their original company fleet numbers as shown here by this view of No 30 in SHMD ownership. Both were withdrawn by the end of 1927. *Barry Cross Collection/Online Transport Archive*

Above: **Although delivered** in 1903 to the Sheeerness & District Electrical Power & Traction Co Ltd (see page 47) – where, presumably, they would have been numbered 9-12 – the four outstanding cars ordered from Brush never entered service and were sold later the same year to the City of Birmingham Tramways Co Ltd, which was another BET subsidiary. Numbered 189-92, the quartet entered service in 1904 and No 189 is illustrated here. Following the expiry of the last of the company's leases on 1 January 1912, one of the quartet was sold for further service with the Devonport & District Tramways Co – as No 30 – with the remaining three being transferred to subsidiaries of the Birmingham & Midland Tramways Joint Committee. The Devonport car was acquired by Plymouth Corporation following its take-over of the company's lines on 2 October 1915, re-entering service – following a period in store – as Plymouth No 70 in 1918; like a number of ex-Devonport cars it was subsequently provided with either a replacement Peckham P22 or Preston Flexible four-wheel truck. *Barry Cross Collection/Online Transport Archive*

Opposite above: **The single** largest batch of tramcars acquired by the Yorkshire Woollen District) Electric Tramways Co Ltd was represented by the forty-two open-top cars – Nos 7-48 – that were supplied Brush on the same manufacturer's type A four-wheel trucks during 1902 and 1903. The company was a subsidiary of BET and, shortly after delivery, three cars – Nos 19, 20 and 29 – were loaned to a second BET subsidiary – the Barnsley & District Electric Traction Co – as they were similar to the Brush cars – No 1-12 – that had already been supplied to Barnsley & District. The trio ran in Barnsley in their Yorkshire (WD) livery and retained their original fleet numbers. Here Yorkshire (WD) No 19 is pictured operating in Cheapside, Barnsley during its brief sojourn to southwards. *Barry Cross Collection/Online Transport Archive*

Opposite below: **Shortly after** their introduction to service with Yorkshire (WD) almost half of the Brush-built cars had been fitted with Bellamy-type top covers. No 20, one of the trio loaned to Barnsley & District, was one of those so modified; the car here is seen in Sheffield Road, Barnsley. All three cars were returned to Yorkshire (WD) by the end of 1904. *Barry Cross Collection/Online Transport Archive*

Above: **Wigan Corporation** was unusual in operating both 3ft 6in and standard gauge trams alongside each other, although the former were gradually converted to standard gauge. Work on conversion in 1904 resulted in the disposal of the corporation's first electric trams – Nos 1-12 acquired from ER&TCW on Peckham four-wheel trucks in 1900 – to the Coventry Electric Tramways Co Ltd (operation was taken over by the corporation on 1 January 1912). In Coventry, the open-top cars were renumbered 19-30 and retained, with two exceptions, open lower-deck vestibules until withdrawal. The two exceptions – Nos 19 and 24 – were fitted with partial enclosed lower-deck vestibules in 1924 and No 19 was further modified – as illustrated in this view outside the corporation's Priestley's Bridge depot – with fully-enclosed lower-deck vestibules in 1930. That year saw a number of the class – Nos 24, 27 and 30 – withdrawn, although Nos 27 and 30 survived out of use until the final closure of the system, due to German bombing, in November 1940. A further four of the batch – Nos 20, 21, 25 and 29 – were all scrapped by the end of 1934. The remaining cars survived in service until final closure on 14 November 1940 and were all scrapped the following year. No 30 was to suffer serious damage as a result of the 14 November raid when the depot was hit. *W.A. Camwell/National Tramway Museum*

Opposite: **The second** operator to acquire a batch of the surplus bogie trams operated by the Gravesend & Northfleet Electric Tramways was the Swansea Improvements & Tramways Co Ltd that took four later in 1904. These were to become Nos 42-45 in South Wales and, in 1924, all four were rebuilt as fully enclosed and fitted with replacement maximum traction bogies constructed by the operator itself; it is in this guise that No 43 is pictured at the Sketty terminus of routes 4 and 5. All four of the rebuilt trams survived to the end of the Swansea system on 29 June 1937. *Barry Cross Collection/Online Transport Archive*

Above: **The Swansea** Improvements & Tramways Co Ltd further supplemented its fleet in 1904 by the purchase of four open-top cars from the Weston-super-Mare & District Electric Supply Co Ltd. These were from two batches of cars – Nos 1-8 of 1902 and 9-12 of 1903 – that Brush supplied on Brill 21E four-wheel trucks and were destined to become Swansea Nos 46-49. Here, No 46 is pictured on St Helens Road in original condition. The four cars were rebuilt by the company in 1922 and fitted with fully enclosed top covers whilst retaining the open lower-deck platforms and, as such, remained in service until the conversion of the Swansea system. *Barry Cross Collection/Online Transport Archive*

Opposite above: **The final** second-hand trams acquired by the Swansea Improvements & Tramways Co Ltd at this time were six single-deck combination cars – Nos 50-55 – that were acquired from the Middleton Electric Traction Co Ltd in 1905. These were the remainder of the batch of ten cars with the other four been sold to the Oldham, Ashton-under-Lyne & Hyde Electric Tramways Co Ltd the previous year. New in 1901, the ten cars were originally built by ER&TCW and fitted with Brill 22E maximum traction bogies. Here, the first of the batch is seen on Oxford Street. The combination cars survived the First World War but were deemed lacking capacity in the post-war years and were withdrawn, a number being replaced by new single-deck cars that carried the same numbers. *Barry Cross Collection/Online Transport Archive*

Opposite below: **When the** 3ft 6in Taunton & West Somerset Electric Railways & Tramways Co Ltd – later the Taunton Electric Traction Co Ltd – first introduced trams to Taunton in August 1901, it employed five open-top double-deck cars supplemented by a sixth supplied the following year; all were constructed by Brush on the same manufacturers A type four-wheel truck. In 1905, with the tramway's operation suspended for road reconstruction, the fleet was replaced by six single-deck cars with the original six cars sold to the 3ft 6in gauge Leamington & Warwick Electrical Co Ltd, which opened on 15 July of that year, where they became Nos 7-12. This side view records one of the sextet outside the company's depot at Eastcote Bridge with one of the original six cars – No 6 (again built by Brush, this time in 1905) – in the background. During the 1920s, a number of the ex-Taunton cars received replacement Peckham P22 trucks. All six second-hand cars survived through to the conversion of the three-mile route to bus operation on 16 August 1930. *Hugh Nicol/National Tramway Museum*

Oxford Street, Swansea

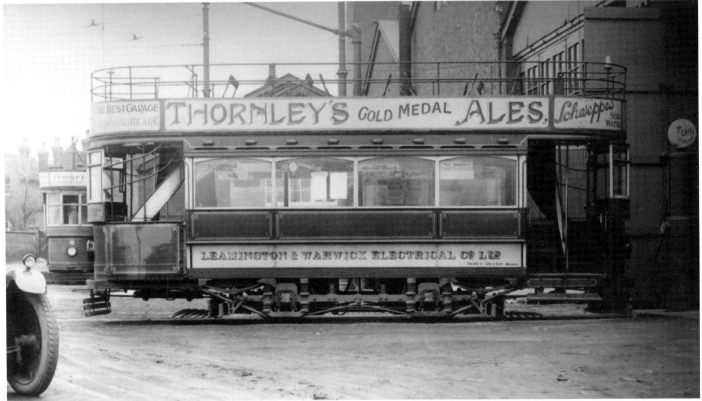

In 1902, Brush supplied Croydon Corporation with five open-top cars fitted with reversed – i.e. smaller wheels leading – Brush BB bogies; Nos 56-60 were not destined to have a long life with the corporation, being sold at £623 apiece to the South Metropolitan Electric Tramways Co Ltd in 1906, where they were designated as Class L. Little alteration was undertaken by the new owners, although the cars showed a tendency to derail on the sharp curve from Tamworth Road into Pitlake. This may have resulted in the reversed bogies being converted into the more usual – larger diameter wheel leading – arrangement on one of the batch (No 27). The fact that no other cars were so modified suggests that the alteration did not resolve the problem. No 27 was the first to be withdrawn – in about 1930 – with the remainder following in 1931. All were scrapped at Fulwell depot in 1934. Here No 29 – ex-Croydon No 58 (i) – is seen on Aurelia Road. *Barry Cross Collection/Online Transport Archive*

In addition to the five ex-Croydon cars acquired in 1906, South Met also acquired four cars from Gravesend & Northfleet the same year. The bogie cars, which had originally been supplied by ERT&CW in 1902 on Brill 22E bogies, had proved too large for the traffic generated on the Gravesend & Northfleet with the result that six of the batch had been sold to Jarrow & District and Swansea Improvements & Tramways Co – like South Met associated BET subsidiaries – in 1904. South Met took the remaining four at £560 each; designating the quartet as Class O, the company renumbered them 30, 32-34. The only South Met trams to be equipped with reversed staircases, No 32 was rebuilt in the mid-1920 with lengthened platforms that permitted non-reversed stairs. All four underwent slight modification at Hendon in 1930, with the upper-deck wire screens being replaced by metal sheeting. No 34 is recorded here on Aurelia Road in original condition. All four cars were withdrawn in 1931 and scrapped at Fulwell three years later. *Barry Cross Collection/Online Transport Archive*

Above: **Yorkshire (Woollen** District) No 59 – a single-deck demi car probably constructed by BEC under licence from Brush on a BEC-built four-wheel truck – was acquired in 1904. Equipped with the patented Raworth regenerative control system, the car was designed to operate within the Heckmondwike UDC area in response to the high electric charges that the council was imposing on the tramway. Introduced to the Heckmondwike to Hightown service, the car – which is seen here at Bradford Road, Millbridge, where the cars had to reverse to complete their journeys – proved successful and later in 1904, further sets of regenerative equipment were ordered. The delivery of these new trams rendered No 59 redundant and, in September 1905, it was loaned to the Barnsley & District Electric Traction Co; it was purchased outright two months later for £500 having proved itself in operation on the short Smithies section. In Barnsley, it became No 13. The final Barnsley trams operated on 3 September 1930. *Barry Cross Collection/Online Transport Archive*

Opposite above: **Farnworth UDC** introduced trams on 9 January 1902 and operated thirteen open-top cars – Nos 1-13 – that had been supplied by G.F. Milnes & Co in two batches; the first eight in 1901 and the remainder the following year. All were fitted with Brill 22E maximum traction bogies. On 1 April 1906, South Lancashire Tramways leased the operation of the UDC's three-mile network and purchased the thirteen trams. These were to become company Nos 46-58. Between 1923 and 1926, all of the batch, with the exception of Nos 51 and 52, received replacement English Electric open-balcony bodies and with all bar Nos 49 and 57 receiving EMB Type A Burnley bogies. No 57, pictured here, had low sideframe Burnley bogies fitted. Following the final conversion of the company's system to bus operation on 16 December 1933, six of the rebuilt cars – Nos 47, 48, 50, 54, 55 and 58 – were sold to Bolton Corporation. *Barry Cross Collection/Online Transport Archive*

Opposite below: **Such was** the rapidity with which the Glasgow Corporation network was converted from horse to electric operation that it outstripped the capabilities of the transport department to construct sufficient new bodies at Coplawhill, thus requiring the purchase of additional bodies from outside contractors. In addition, it was decided to undertake the conversion of a number of ex-horse tram bodies to electric traction as many of these bodies were less than a decade old. Although there were issues with the wooden framing that resulted in many cars being scrapped, a total of 120 were converted between 1899 and 1903 with all being fitted with Brill 21E four-wheel trucks. A typical example is pictured here alongside 'Standard' No 141. The first four to be withdrawn, in March 1909, were Nos 24, 32, 47 and 116, which were sold to the Dumbarton Burgh & County Tramways. This company operated a route that connected to the corporation line to Dalmuir West to Balloch, paralleling the railway line, with branches to Dumbarton and Jamestown. The quartet, which became company Nos 27-30, were acquired to operate the Jamestown extension, which opened in early 1909, as this section included a low bridge; when operating on the Jamestown section, the four cars were effectively used as single-deckers through the simple expediency of blocking access to the upper deck. All four were still in service when the last Dumbarton trams operated on 3 March 1928. *Barry Cross Collection/Online Transport Archive*

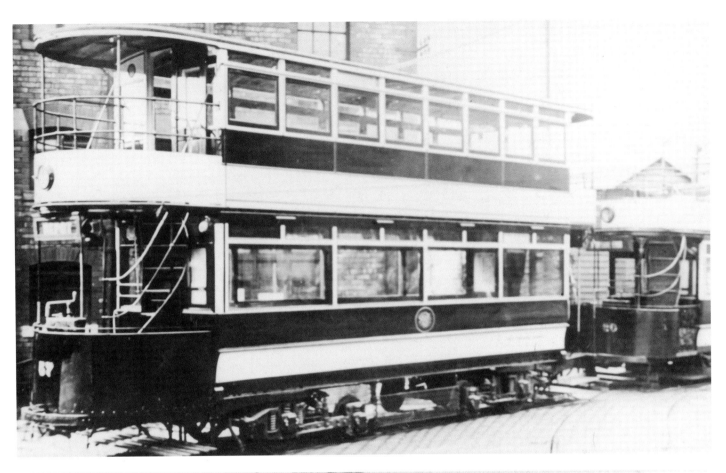

In order to replace the two bogie trams that Gravesend & Northfleet sold to Jarrow & District, two four-wheel open-top cars that had been built for the latter – Nos 5 and 6 – were acquired by the former in 1908, retaining their original numbers. Nos 5 and 6 were part of a batch of eight cars – Nos 1-8 – supplied to Jarrow & District by Brush for the opening of the system on 29 November 1906. Fitted with Brush-built AA trucks, the two cars survived until the final closure of the Gravesend system on 28 February 1929. In October 1928, one of the duo – No 5 – is pictured in the company's depot at Northfleet. *Hugh Nicol/National Tramway Museum*

Opposite above: For the opening of the Norwich Electric Traction Co, a subsidiary of the New General Traction Co, Brush supplied forty open-top cars – Nos 1-40 – fitted with M&G Radial four-wheel trucks. These were all fitted with two 25hp motors with the exception of Nos 7, 9, 16, 32 and 36 that had two 30hp motors and, in 1910, these five cars were transferred to the Coventry Electric Tramways Co, another subsidiary of the New General Traction Co. Renumbered 37-41 in Coventry, the cars were fitted with canopies over the lower-deck vestibules before entering service. In 1916, all five received replacement Peckham P22 four-wheel trucks but were otherwise to remain unaltered – as shown in this view of No 38 (ex-Norwich No 16) on Broadgate. All five were to survive through to the final demise of the Coventry system in November 1940, being scrapped the following year. *Barry Cross Collection/Online Transport Archive*

Opposite below: Between 1906 and 1908, the Mexborough & Swinton Tramways Co was supplied with twenty trams; all were built by Brush. Nos 1-16 were open-top and fitted with M&G Radial four-wheel trucks whilst Nos 17-20 were fitted with open-balcony top covers from new; this quartet was equipped with Brill 21E four-wheel trucks. Traffic on the system – which opened on 6 February 1907 – was lighter than anticipated with the result that the company sold two of the open-top cars – Nos 10 and 14 – to the wonderfully named Dewsbury, Ossett & Soothill Nether Tramway in 1911, where they became Nos 10 and 9 respectively. No 14 briefly operated with Mexborough & Swinton with a top cover but both were sold – for a total of £860 – in open-top condition retaining their original trucks; the latter were subsequently replaced by Brill 21E trucks. In 1922, both were fitted with new open-balcony top covers and it is in this condition that the pair were recorded at the company's Ossett depot. In 1928, as the Mexborough system was progressively converted to trolleybus operation, a further two cars – Nos 7 and 15 – were sold for a total of £100 to the Dewsbury company; these had been fitted before the First World War with open-balcony top covers and had also received replacement Brush-built 21E trucks between 1919 and 1923. These two were to become Nos 11 and 12 respectively with their new owners. The Dewsbury company, which was part of the National Electric Construction Co, was – along with other subsidiaries – to pass to BET ownership in 1931 with operational control thereafter in the hands of the BET subsidiary Yorkshire (Woollen District). The new operators decided to convert the Dewsbury system to bus operation with the last trams operating on 19 October 1933; the ex-Mexborough quartet were scrapped after the conversion. *Hugh Nicol/National Tramway Museum*

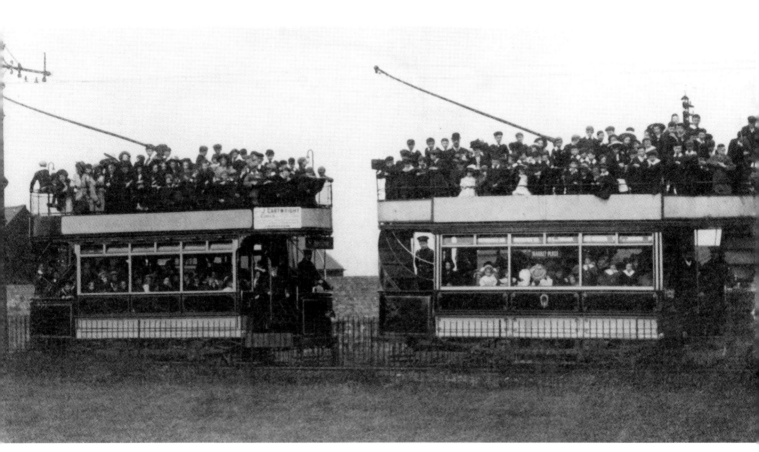

Opposite above: **The last** tram acquired by the Jarrow & District Electric Tramways Co Ltd was No 10, which is seen here on the right alongside No 3 (one of the original batch of eight supplied by Brush in 1906 of which two were sold to the Gravesend & Northfleet Electric Tramways Ltd in 1907 – see page 32). No 10 had originally been Gateshead & District Tramways Co No 35 and was new in 1901 as one of a batch of 25 – Nos 21-45 – open-top cars supplied by ER&TCW on Brill 21E four-wheel trucks, Initially, the car was loaned to Jarrow & District but was subsequently purchased. Its exact date of transfer is uncertain but it featured in the rolling stock returns of 31 December 1911. It probably retained its Gateshead fleet number initially before becoming No 10 by 1914. The Jarrow & District ceased tramway operation on 30 June 1929. *Barry Cross Collection/Online Transport Archive*

Opposite below: **For the** electrification of its route to the north of Belfast on 12 February 1906, the Cavehill & Whitewell Tramway Co – latterly a BET subsidiary –acquired 10 open-top cars from Brush – Nos 1-10 – in two batches; Nos 6-10 were larger and fitted with Brush Conaty radial four-wheel trucks. When Belfast Corporation took over ownership and operation of the Cavehill & Whitewell tramway on 1 June 1911, it sold two of these larger cars to the Mansfield & District Light Railway Co the following year. Remaining open-top and unvestibuled through their career in the East Midlands, the two cars were eventually to receive replacement Peckham P22 four-wheel trucks. The two cars became Mansfield & District Nos 19 and 20 and here the former is pictured on the Chesterfield Road route. The last Mansfield & District trams operated on 9 October 1932. *Maurice O'Connor/National Tramway Museum*

Below: **Following the** final demise of the City of Birmingham Tramways Co Ltd on 1 January 1912, its fleet was largely transferred to the operators – Birmingham Corporation and Birmingham & Midland Tramways Joint Committee – which had taken over the company's network. However, a number – including one of the ex-Sheerness cars (see page 46) – passed to the Devonport & District Tramways Co. During 1904 and 1905, Brush had supplied City of Birmingham with thirty-six open-top cars on Brush Conaty four-wheel trucks; Nos 217-38/43-56 – of which No 229 is pictured in Whitton depot – were known as the 'Aston' class and four of the type were transferred to Devonport & District in 1912, where they became Nos 26-29. Remaining open-top, the quartet were in service when Plymouth Corporation took over Devonport & District on 2 October 1915. The quartet were renumbered as Plymouth Nos 66-69 and were amongst fifteen of the ex-company cars used from the take-over; like a number of ex-company cars, they were eventually re-equipped with either Peckham P22 or Preston Flexible four-wheel trucks. *Barry Cross Collection/Online Transport Archive*

Above: **The final** trams acquired in 1912 by the Devonport & District Tramways Co from the City of Birmingham Tramways Co Ltd were three of the 'Bristol Road' class that became Nos 31-33 in Devon. The 'Bristol Road' cars comprised two batches: the first fifteen, Nos 151-65, were supplied by ER&TCW in 1901 with the remaining six, Nos 166-71, being completed by the company itself during 1901 and 1902. All were open-top cars, as shown in this view of No 162 when new in 1901, and were fitted with Peckham 9A four-wheel cantilever trucks. As with the remainder of the Devonport & District fleet, the trio passed to Plymouth Corporation on 2 October 1915 eventually becoming Nos 71-73. As with other ex-Devonport cars, three cars were re-equipped with either Peckham P22 or Preston Flexible four-wheel trucks. Nos 71 and 73 were renumbered 41 and 42 respectively in 1922. *Barry Cross Collection/Online Transport Archive*

Opposite above: **In 1912,** Barking Town UDC Light Railways acquired its last new tram; this was an open-balcony car supplied by Brush on a Peckham P22 four-wheel truck. The car, fitted for operation over the LCC conduit system as well as conventional overhead, was obtained for use on the through service from Aldgate to Loxford Bridge inaugurated on 20 December 1912. However, the financial results of the through service were not the success that the council anticipated with the result that it withdrew from the agreement on 31 December 1914. This left No 10 – along with Nos 8 and 9 delivered in 1911 (supplied by Brush but this time on Peckham R7A radial four-wheel trucks) – as surplus to requirements. No 8 was initially loaned to Ilford Corporation – as No 28 – in 1915 and subsequently bought for £460 with No 10 being sold for £650, becoming Ilford No 27 in 1914. The latter is illustrated here in the corporation's depot on Ley Street. No 28 was withdrawn and scrapped in 1930 whilst No 27 survived to become LPTB No 31 in July 1933. It was withdrawn in 1938 and subsequently scrapped. *Barry Cross Collection/Online Transport Archive*

Opposite below: **Similar in** design to the same manufacturer's 'M' class trams supplied to the LCC, Hurst Nelson supplied a batch of six open-balcony cars – Nos 53-58 – to the Paisley District Tramways Co in 1911. Fitted with the same manufacturer's swing-bolster four-wheel trucks, the six were also initially fitted – as was usual practice in London – with two trolleypoles; one of these was quickly removed in Paisley. The original five were delivered with open lower-deck vestibules but No 58 was completed with enclosed vestibules. The ride quality of these cars was poor, leading to complaints and, despite modification by Hurst Nelson, all were withdrawn in 1914. Sold to Dundee Corporation for £350 – without motors and controllers – each, two re-entered service in August 1914 and the remaining four in February the following year. Numbered 69-74 in Dundee, Nos 73 and 74 were renumbered 67 and 68 in 1927 – taking the numbers previously carried by Dundee's shortlived trolleybuses – whilst No 68 received a replacement Brill 21E truck in 1929. All six were withdrawn in 1930 and scrapped. *Barry Cross Collection/Online Transport Archive*

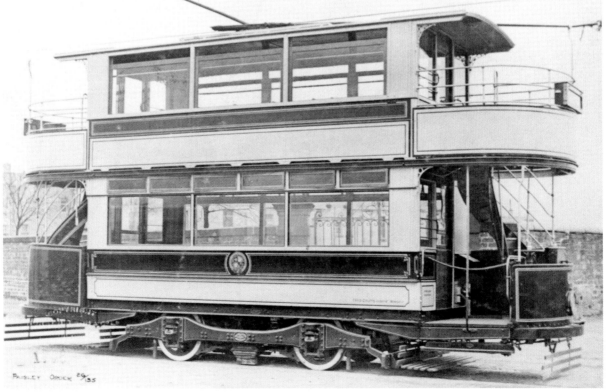

Above: **As elsewhere,** the First World War resulted in an increase in traffic on the tramways operated by Bexley UDC and as a result, in 1915, the council hired six 'B' class trams from the LCC; these were probably allocated Bexley Nos 17-22. The LCC had withdrawn a significant number of the type from 1912 onwards and so were able to provide these cars from store. Five additional cars – Bexley Nos 23-27 – were acquired in 1917 and a final twelve – Bexley Nos 28-39 – were obtained in 1918 following the creation of the Bexley UDC & Dartford Light Railways Joint Committee after the disastrous fire of 6 August 1917 when the entire Dartford fleet was destroyed in a depot fire. Nos 17-20 were returned to the LCC in 1919 along with No 22, exchanged for LCC No 128. The following year, No 26 – in lieu of No 21 – was returned. It is not clear which 'B' class cars in total were used by Bexley but Nos 109/11/12/20/28/30/39/40/51/57/67/78 /80/84/87/96 and 201 are recorded as having finally been sold to Bexley. Various renumberings took place with the result that eventually the seventeen cars were Nos 17-33. All survived to become part of the LPTB fleet in July 1933 but were destined to be withdrawn and scrapped by the end of that year. Here, No 30 is pictured at Horn's Cross in 1929. *Barry Cross Collection/Online Transport Archive*

Opposite above: **Oldham Corporation** acquired from ER&TCW ten 28-seat single-deck cars – Nos 17-26 – on Brill 21E four-wheel trucks in 1902; in 1915 one was sold to the Great Grimsby Street Tramways Co, becoming No 38 on Humberside. Used by the company as a private hire tram primarily, it was one of the company-owned trams that passed to Cleethorpes UDC when that authority acquired the remaining assets of the company on 15 July 1936 (Grimsby Corporation had acquired its part of the company's network on 6 April 1925). It was to be repainted in dark blue and primrose by Cleethorpes; this was intended to be the livery for the trams but No 38 was the only one so treated as the remaining trams were withdrawn on 17 July 1937. No 38 acted as the official last tram. It is seen here outside the Pelham Road depot that Cleethorpes UDC also acquired from the company in 1936. *Barry Cross Collection/Online Transport Archive*

Opposite below: **In 1902,** the Rothesay Tramways Co Ltd acquired a batch of five crossbench cars – Nos 11-15 – with open end compartments from ER&TCW. These were fitted with Brill 22E maximum traction bogies as shown in this side view taken in about 1904. In 1915 two of the batch – Nos 11 and 12 – were transferred, without bogies, to the Greenock & Port Glasgow Tramways Co where, it is suggested, that they became Nos 47 and 48, having been equipped with replacement Brush B maximum traction bogies. The last Greenock & Port Glasgow Tramways cars operated on 15 July 1929. The three remaining cars in Rothesay were all fitted with enclosed vestibules in 1919 although Nos 13 and 14 were converted again to open vestibule in the early 1930s. *D.W.K. Jones Collection/ Online Transport Archive*

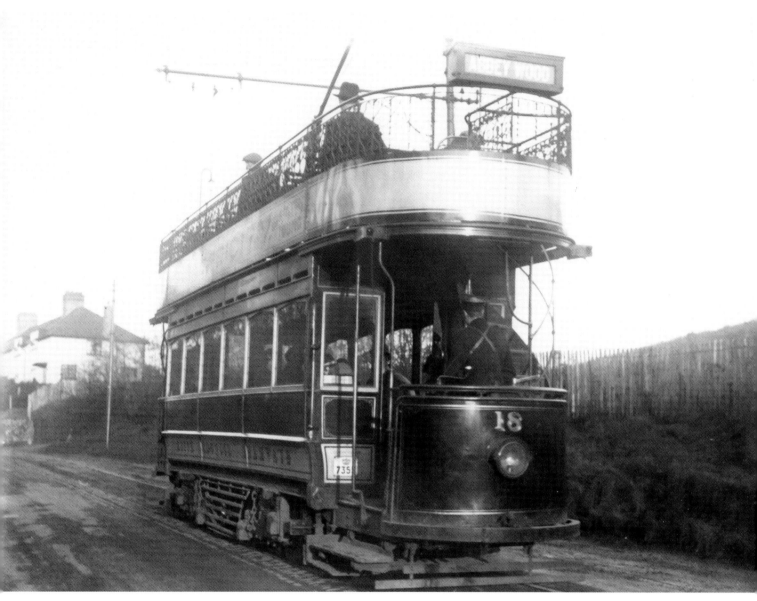

Above: **In 1916,** in order to supplement its fleet to cater for the increased traffic caused by the First World War, Erith UDC initially hired four 'W' class open-top trams from LUT. It is possible that a number of cars were involved initially but, eventually, four of the batch – Nos 187, 192, 221 and 252 – were acquired. These were originally all built by G.F. Milnes & Co with the exception of No 221, which was constructed by BEC; all were fitted with Brill 22E bogies. Initially, as they lacked track brakes, they were not permitted to operate on the gradient in Bexley Road. Magnetic brakes were fitted in 1922; at the same time the bodies were modified to include full-length canopies over the lower-deck vestibules and altered staircases. This is the condition in which No 18 is seen at Barnehurst on 19 January 1929. The quartet survived to become Nos 15D-18D following the creation of the LPTB but were withdrawn three months later; they were scrapped at Brixton Hill during the summer of 1934 never having been repainted into the LPTB livery. *Hugh Nicol/National Tramway Museum*

Opposite above: **In 1900,** Hull Corporation acquired its only bogie car; this was No 101 that was built by G.F. Milnes & Co and fitted with Brill 22E bogies. Towards the end of the decade, the car was fitted with a short top cover – as shown in this view – and its seating was increased from sixty-nine to seventy. In 1916, the tram was acquired by Erith UDC for £400 in order again to cater for the increased wartime traffic. Before the car entered service – still in its Hull livery but renumbered 19 – the tram had received second-hand wheels from LUT to replace its unusual centre flange set. Nicknamed the 'Tank', No 19 was to become LPTB No 19D in July 1933 but was withdrawn later that year and scrapped at Brixton Hill early the following year. *Hugh Nicol/National Tramway Museum*

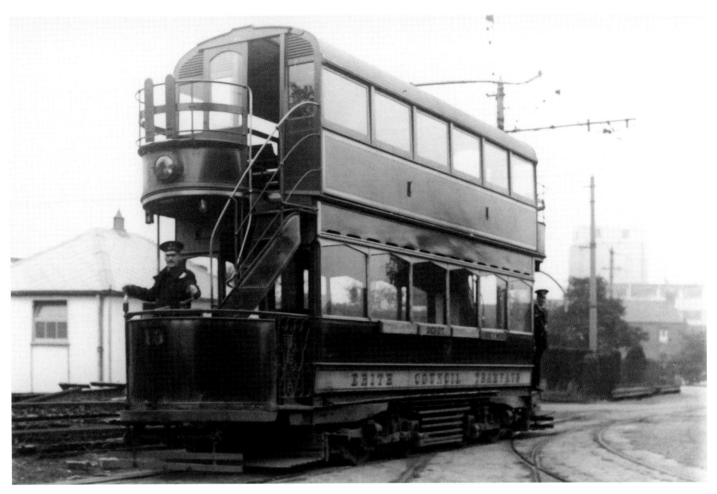

In 1908, the Greenock & Port Glasgow Tramways Co took delivery of a single demi-car No 40 – seen here when new – from UEC. The tram was originally fitted with a Brill 21E 4ft 7¾in-gauge four-wheel truck. The narrative for this tram is not consistent but it would appear that the car was sold in 1916 to the Rothesay Tramways Co Ltd and, following the conversion of its truck to 3ft 6in gauge, was used, as No 21, for a period on a service from the depot at Pointhouse to Ettrick Bay. In early 1920, the manager proved an estimate for reusing the truck and frames of No 21 to construct a new four-wheel toastrack car – No 22 – that entered service by 1923. The original body of No 21 was retained for a period at Ettrick Bay. *D.W.K. Jones Collection/Online Transport Archive*

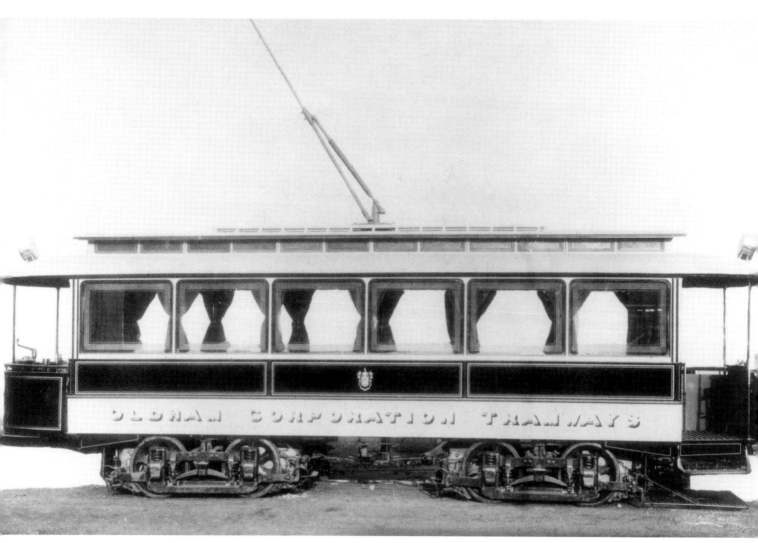

In 1900, Oldham Corporation acquired four trams – two single-deck and two double-deck – for evaluation purposes prior to ordering significant numbers for its new operations. No 4 was a single-deck car supplied by ER&TCW on Brill 27G bogies. In 1902, the same manufacturer supplied a further twelve similar cars – Nos 5-16 – but the following year No 13 was rebuilt as a double-decker. The remaining twelve single-deck bogie cars were all withdrawn in 1916 and sold to Rotherham Corporation where they became Nos 38-49. One of the batch – No 44 – was destroyed by fire in 1918. In 1919, eight of the batch were withdrawn and sold to Walthamstow Corporation. In 1921, one of the survivors was retrucked with a Cravens-supplied four-wheel truck and was renumbered 28 (ii). In 1923, the other two were shortened from 35ft 0in to 30ft 6in and also refitted with a Cravens-built four-wheel truck; these two may have been renumbered 49 and 50 at the same time but were certainly to become Nos 16 (ii) and 17 (ii) when the original cars with these numbers were withdrawn (by 1923). These three cars were all withdrawn in 1929. This view records one of the bogie cars whilst with its original owner. *D.W.K. Jones Collection/Online Transport Archive*

In April 1903, the first of 100 'B' class trams – Nos 102-201 – entered service with the LCC. These had been supplied by ER&TCW and were fitted with Brill 21E four-wheel trucks. Delivered as open-top cars and – as was required by Metropolitan Police regulations – open lower-deck vestibules, a number were fitted with fully-enclosed top covers. The type was not wholly successful in operation; structural weakness and a predilection for the use of the newer – and larger – bogie cars resulted in a number of the 'B' class being relegated to rush hour work only and, by the outbreak of the First World War, many were in store. From 1915 until 1918, following agreement with the relevant government departments, more than half of the batch were either hired initially (as with some of those acquired by Bexley) or sold, with batches being bought by Newport, Rotherham, Sheffield and Southampton corporations. Typical of the type is No 115 seen here; this was one of the cars eventually sold during the war (it passed to either Newport or Rotherham). Although none of the cars acquired by other operators survives, similar car No 106, which was converted into a snowbroom (No 022) in 1925, was preserved on withdrawal and has been restored to original condition. It is now based at the National Tramway Museum. *Barry Cross Collection/Online Transport Archive*

Above: **Sheffield Corporation** acquired the single largest number of redundant LCC 'B' class cars in 1917, purchasing a total of twenty; these were LCC Nos 103/08/16/19/21/26/49/52/56/60/66/70/71/73/79/81/85/86/88/93. In Sheffield, the trams became Nos 56, 94, 125/29/87/88, 203/07/08/10 and 356-65. Of these, Nos 56, 94, 125 and 129 were supplied as bodies only and were fitted with Peckham P22 four-wheel trucks before re-entering service. No 56 was renumbered 128 in 1924 and No 94 became No 90 the following year. This view records Sheffield No 188 which had originally been LCC No 186. Of this batch of second-hand cars, thirteen were withdrawn between 1926 and 1928 with the remainder following in 1931. In addition to these twenty cars, Sheffield also acquired, in 1926, the eight 'B' class cars – Nos 40-47 (ii) – that Rotherham Corporation had acquired in 1917; six of these re-entered service in Sheffield as Nos 91-6 with the other two cars being scrapped. These six cars, which had been converted into open-balcony by Rotherham, were all withdrawn in 1931. *Barry Cross Collection/Online Transport Archive*

Opposite: **One of** the purchasers of the redundant 'B' class cars was Newport Corporation, which acquired six of the cars fitted with enclosed top covers in 1917. The cars that headed to South Wales were six from the following: Nos 105/14/15/27/36/37/42/59/64 (those that did not get sold to Newport were amongst those acquired by Rotherham Corporation at the same time). The six cars, which effectively cost £580 apiece, became Nos 45-50 in the Newport fleet and here No 48 is pictured at the Corporation Road terminus in 1934. The batch was originally allocated to the service between Pillgwenlly and Clarence Place to cater for the numbers employed on war work. The first Newport trams to operate with top covers, the cars were initially limited to that route due to low railway bridges elsewhere. No 49 was later fitted with lower-deck vestibules whilst, in the late 1920s, No 47 was slightly reduced in height; this work was subsequently undertaken on the remainder of the batch so that the trams were capable of passing under the low bridges. The final Newport trams operated on 5 September 1937. *Barry Cross Collection/Online Transport Archive*

Above: On 5 March 1917, the Yorkshire (West Riding) Electric Tramways Ltd suffered a catastrophic fire at its Castleford depot, which resulted in the destruction of eight passenger cars plus the works car. In order to supplement its existing fleet, the company hired eight cars from Leeds Corporation in 1917; these were Nos 133/38/47/48/63/70/77/80 and were part of a batch of fifty cars – Nos 133-82 – that had been supplied to the corporation by Brush in 1899. Fitted with Peckham Cantilever four-wheel trucks, the cars had originally been open-top but were equipped with short top covers before the First World War. The eight cars, which had been nicknamed 'Bathing Huts' in Leeds, were formally bought – at £800 apiece – by the company in 1919. Numbered 68-75 by the company, withdrawals commenced in 1925 but at least two of the batch – Nos 70 and 74 – were still in service when the last of the company's routes were converted to bus operation on 25 July 1932. Here, No 71 is pictured heading through the Bull Ring in Wakefield as Queen Victoria looks on. *Barry Cross Collection/Online Transport Archive*

Opposite: The first electric tramway to be closed in Britain was that which served Sheerness in Kent. The Sheerness & District Electrical Power & Traction Co Ltd opened its 2½ mile 3ft 6in gauge line on 9 April 1903, using eight open-top four-wheel cars supplied by Brush on the same manufacturer's A trucks. A further four cars were also delivered but never used and were sold later the same year to the City of Birmingham Tramways Co Ltd. Owned by BET, the Achilles' heel of the system – other than traffic not living up to expectations – was that much of the equipment used – including the bow collectors as seen on this view of No 5 – was supplied by the German company Siemens. As a result, when the First World War broke out in August 1914, supplies of spare parts dried up. Due to these various factors, the tramway closed suddenly on 7 July 1917. The eight trams were acquired the following year by Darlington Corporation; six re-entered service – as Nos 19-24 – with their bow collectors replaced by conventional trolleypoles whilst the remaining two cars were dismantled for spares. Their second career was destined to be even shorter than their first, as Darlington decided to convert its 3ft 6in gauge tramway to trolleybus operation; the last trams operated on 10 April 1926. *Barry Cross Collection/ Online Transport Archive*

Above: Southampton Corporation was another purchaser of 'B' class cars from the LCC; six were acquired in 1918, becoming Nos 75-80 on the South Coast. Although these had been fitted with enclosed top-deck covers, Southampton removed these during 1922 in order to permit operation through the Bargate; although this obstruction was bypassed in two phases during the 1930s, the six ex-LCC cars were never re-equipped with top covers and remained open-top until withdrawal. One of the six was withdrawn in 1934; the other five survived into the post-war era but all had been withdrawn for scrap by the end of 1948. Pictured outside Portswood depot on 19 May 1946 is No 80. *John Meredith Collection/Online Transport Archive*

Opposite above: Sheffield Corporation purchased between 1899 and 1904 a total of sixty-nine single-deck cars; these were all withdrawn by 1921 but a number were to find their way to other operators. Nos 53-58 were supplied by ER&TCW in 1900 on Brill 21E four-wheel trucks. No 56 – seen here whilst in service with Sheffield – was one of the first to be sold; it was acquired in 1918 by the Glossop Tramways Ltd, a subsidiary of the Urban Electric Supply Co Ltd (which also owned the Camborne & Redruth). The car became Glossop No 9; this was the last tram acquired by the company and all nine trams operated by the company were to be withdrawn when the 4½ mile route was converted to bus operation on 24 December 1927. *Barry Cross Collection/Online Transport Archive*

Opposite below: In 1918, the Musselburgh & District Electric Light & Traction Co Ltd acquired three ex-Sheffield Corporation single-deck cars. These were Sheffield Nos 94, 203 and 210 which were to become company Nos 17-19 respectively. No 17 was originally was built by Brush in 1900, whilst Nos 18 and 19 were originally built by Sheffield Corporation itself in 1902; all three were fitted with Brill 21E four-wheel trucks. Here is No 17 is at the Joppa terminus with Edinburgh Corporation No 210. The latter car was one of 20 cable-operated cars – No 209-28 – that were originally built in 1902 by ER&TCW in 1902 for the Edinburgh & District Tramways Co Ltd. Originally open-top, the batch was fitted with top covers in 1907. The corporation took over the company's network on 1 July 1919 and the cable lines were electrified. The last trams operated by Musselburgh & District ceased on 31 March 1928. *Barry Cross Collection/Online Transport Archive*

Above: **Another purchaser** of ex-Sheffield Corporation single-deck cars was Preston Corporation, which acquired six – ex-Sheffield Nos 125, 129, 187, 188, 207 and 209 – in 1918 for £350 apiece. The six were to become Preston Nos 40-45. Here, Sheffield No 209 is pictured at Springvale; this was one of a batch of twelve cars – Nos 200-11 – that were constructed by Sheffield Corporation itself on Brill 21E four-wheel trucks in 1903. In Preston, the six cars were to be fitted with enclosed vestibules. At one stage, Preston contemplated converting them to double-deck but the frames were inadequate for this work to be undertaken. However, Nos 40 and 42 – plus some older cars – were withdrawn between 1925 and 1927 and parts used for the construction of three fully-enclosed cars (Nos 30 [ii], 40 [ii] and 42 [ii]). *Barry Cross Collection/Online Transport Archive*

Opposite above: **Four of** the ex-Sheffield Corporation single-deck cars – Nos 91, 93, 103 and 211 – were sold to the Yorkshire (Woollen District) Electric Tramways Co Ltd in November 1919. These had originally been new in 1900 and built by Brush on Brill 21E four-wheel trucks or, in the case of No 211, by the corporation itself, again on a Brill 21E truck, in 1903. The four cars were destined to become Yorkshire Nos 70-73. Here the corporation built example is seen in operation in its home city. *Barry Cross Collection/Online Transport Archive*

Opposite below: **In 1919,** in order to alleviate a shortage of serviceable trams, Walthamstow Corporation acquired eight single-deck cars – the only single-deckers that the corporation operated – from Rotherham Corporation. Fitted with Brill 27G bogies, the cars were part of a batch of twelve cars that Rotherham had acquired in 1916 from Oldham Corporation; they had originally been built in 1902 by ER&TCW. In Walthamstow, the eight cars became Nos 39-46. Four of the batch – Nos 41, 42, 44 and 45 – underwent modernisation in 1925; the remaining four cars were to be withdrawn in 1932 and, following the withdrawal of the ex-LUT cars, the surviving quartet were renumbered 47-50 and it is in this guise that No 50 is seen in this view. The four survivors passed to the LPTB in July 1933 and were notionally renumbered 2062-65; all four were withdrawn and scrapped in 1934. *D.W.K. Jones Collection/Online Transport Archive*

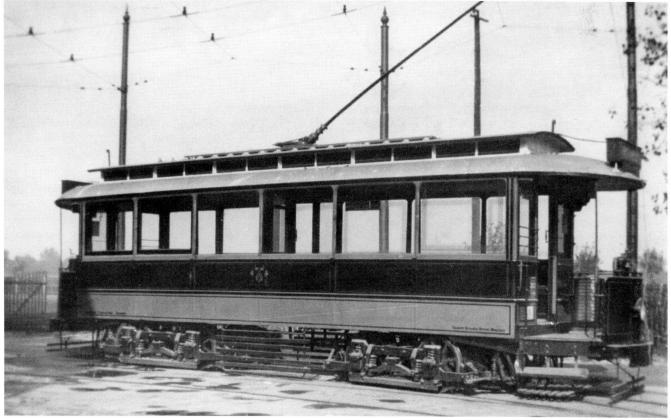

Above: In 1919, Walthamstow Corporation hired six 'W' class bogie cars from LUT; they were purchased the following year. The cars had originally been LUT Nos 226-30/32 and had been built by BEC in 1902 on Brill 22E bogies. As built, they were uncanopied and open-top and they remained in this guise through their career in East London. Renumbered Nos 47-52, the cars were primarily employed on the Markhouse Road route. No 47 and 48, which were in a poor condition, were scrapped in 1930 having been cannibalised for spares; the remaining six cars were all withdrawn in 1932. Here No 50 is pictured at Bell Corner, Walthamstow, with a service – once the policemen have got out of the way! – to Bakers Arms. *Barry Cross Collection/Online Transport Archive*

Opposite above: **Ilkeston Corporation** operated a 4¼ mile 3ft 6in gauge tramway between 16 May 1903 and 16 November 1916, when operation was taken over by the Nottinghamshire & Derbyshire Tramways Co (a Balfour Beatty subsidiary). A total of thirteen open-top trams passed to the new operator; of these Nos 1-9 were supplied originally by ER&TCW on Brill 21E four-wheel trucks in 1902. Of these, two cars were sold in 1919 to the Dunfermline & District Tramways Co (another Balfour Beatty subsidiary), where they became Nos 44 and 45. This view records one of the batch – No 5 – in operation in Bath Street, Ilkeston, shortly after the system opened. A further three of the batch were sold to the City of Carlisle Electric Tramways Co Ltd (see page 57). The two cars sold to Dunfermline & District were withdrawn by 1925, when they were replaced by two trams from Wemyss & District. *Barry Cross Collection/Online Transport Archive*

Opposite below: **LUT acquired** an additional batch of fifty open-top bogie cars from G.F. Milnes & Co – Nos 101-50 – in 1901 – that were fitted with McGuire Type 3 maximum traction bogies primarily for the Uxbridge Road services. Six of the batch – Nos 108/15/25/37/49/50 – were sold in 1919 to Blackpool Corporation, without motors or controllers, for £425 apiece. Following modification, the sextet entered service – still in open-top condition – as No 93-98 as illustrated here in this view of No 97. The ex-LUT cars survived until 1934 when they were scrapped. *D.W.K. Jones Collection/Online Transport Archive*

In 1920, the Yorkshire (Woollen District) Electric Tramways Co Ltd acquired a second batch of single-deck trams from Sheffield Corporation to follow on from the four bought the previous year. All were fitted with Brill 21E four-wheel trucks although one was initially obtained with a Peckham Cantilever four-wheel truck, the eight cars became company Nos 74-81. The original Sheffield Nos 40, 44, 45, 47 and 49 (all built by G.F. Milnes & Co in 1899), 101 (built by Brush in 1901), 128 and 204 (both built by Sheffield Corporation itself during 1902 and 1903). No 81 was renumbered 65 in 1924. Here, Yorkshire (WD) No 74 is pictured on 11 July 1932. Three of the Milnes-built cars – Nos 40, 44 and 49 – had been fitted with enclosed vestibules in Sheffield during 1914 and 1915; these were removed by the corporation prior to transfer to the company. It is probable that this was because the company permitted the use of the rear open platform by smokers. The final company trams operated on 31 October 1934. *Hugh Nicol/National Tramway Museum*

For the opening of the 3ft 6in gauge Chester Corporation system on 6 April 1903, G.F. Milnes & Co supplied 12 open-top cars on Brill 21E four-wheel trucks. No 6 is illustrated here heading towards General station along City Road. Following the system's closure on 15 February 1930, the body of sister car No 4 was acquired by the late Harry Dibdin and stored for many years in his garden. Believed scrapped, the remains were rediscovered in 2005 and are now under restoration by the Hooton Park Trust. *John Meredith Collection/Online Transport Archive*

On 1 January 1920, Barrow Corporation assumed ownership and operation of the BET-owned Barrow-in-Furness Tramways Co Ltd. In order to supplement the existing fleet, which was in a poor condition by the end of the company era (with six of the fleet of twenty-five beyond economic repair), the corporation acquired a number of second-hand trams during that year as a stop-gap measure whilst an order for twelve new single-deck cars was completed. The first to be acquired, in June 1920, were the bodies of four single-deck combination cars from Southport Corporation; these were to become Barrow No 1 (ii) to 4 (ii). The quartet were part of a batch of six – Nos 1, 3, 5, 7, 9 and 11 – supplied by ER&TCW to Southport in 1900. Their original standard gauge Brill 21E four-wheel trucks were replaced by equivalent 4ft 0in gauge trucks before re-entering service in Barrow. Two of the batch – Nos 2 and 3 – were eventually to become works cars in Barrow. All four were withdrawn in 1930. This view records Southport No 1 in operation on the Inner Circle route in Lord Street prior to its transfer. The numbers of the quartet sold to Barrow are unrecorded; of the remaining three cars left in Southport, two were withdrawn and one survived to be reconditioned in 1927, when it was renumbered 45. *Ian L. Cormack Collection/Online Transport Archive*

Barrow Corporation also acquired six single-deck cars from Sheffield Corporation in September 1920; re-gauged to 4ft 0in, these cars became Nos 29-34. The six, all equipped with Brill 21E four-wheel trucks, were originally Sheffield Nos 41 and 43, which had been built by G.F. Milnes & Co in 1899, Nos 100 and 102, which were constructed by Brush in 1902, and Nos 126 and 206, which were built by Sheffield itself in 1901 and 1902 respectively. One of the sextet is pictured here crossing the Walney Bridge, from Walney Island, with an inbound service. *Barry Cross Collection/ Online Transport Archive*

A close-up of one of the ex-Sheffield cars in service with Barrow Corporation. Initially, the cars re-entered service in their Sheffield livery but this was replaced by the corporation's new olive green and cream livery from 1921. Following the rejection of a proposal to modernise the tramway, the system was converted to bus operation, with the last trams being operated on 5 April 1932. *Barry Cross Collection/Online Transport Archive*

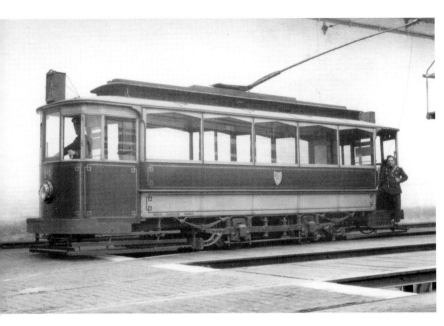

Following on from its purchase of six single-deck cars from Sheffield Corporation in 1918, Preston Corporation acquired a further three in 1920; these were Nos 46-48. Built by Brush in 1900 on Brill 21E four-wheel trucks as Sheffield Nos 89, 90 and 95, the trio had – like the six acquired two years earlier – originally been constructed with open vestibules but a number received extended platforms and enclosed vestibules in Preston. No 48 was renumbered 12 in 1929. One of the trio – No 46 – is pictured here in the corporation's Deepdale Road depot. The final Preston trams operated on 15 December 1935. *Hugh Nicol/ National Tramway Museum*

On 16 May 1903, Ilkeston Corporation introduced 3ft 6in trams to the town; the 4¼ mile system with its thirteen trams passed to the Balfour-Beatty-owned Nottinghamshire & Derbyshire Tramways Co on 16 November 1916. Three of the fleet – numbers unknown – were transferred to another Balfour Beatty subsidiary – the City of Carlisle Electric Tramways Co Ltd – in 1920. One of these is generally believed to have become No 13 (ii) in Cumbria; this was one of the original batch of nine cars supplied by ER&TCW in 1902 on Brill 21E four-wheel trucks. The provenance of the other two cars – Nos 14 (ii) and 15 (ii) that were new in 1925 and 1923 respectively – suggests that both were fitted with new English Electric bodies on ex-Ilkeston trucks. No 12 (ii) was the last tram acquired by City of Carlisle and is seen here outside the depot on London Road on 10 May 1931 some six months before the system was finally converted to bus operation (on the following 21 November). *Hugh Nicol/National Tramway Museum*

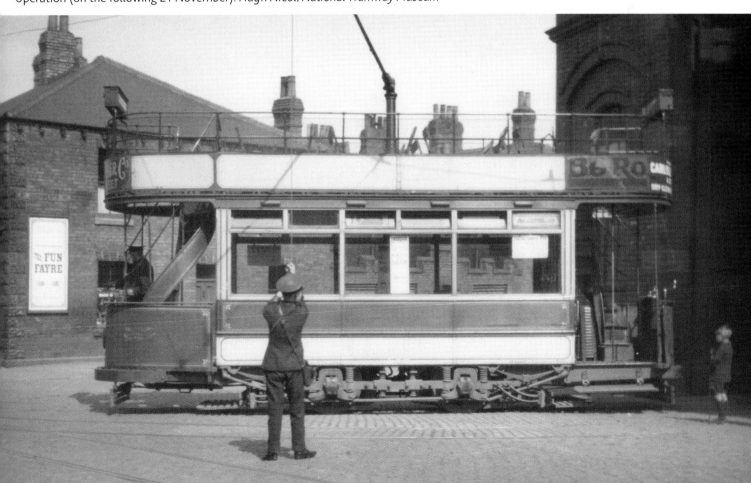

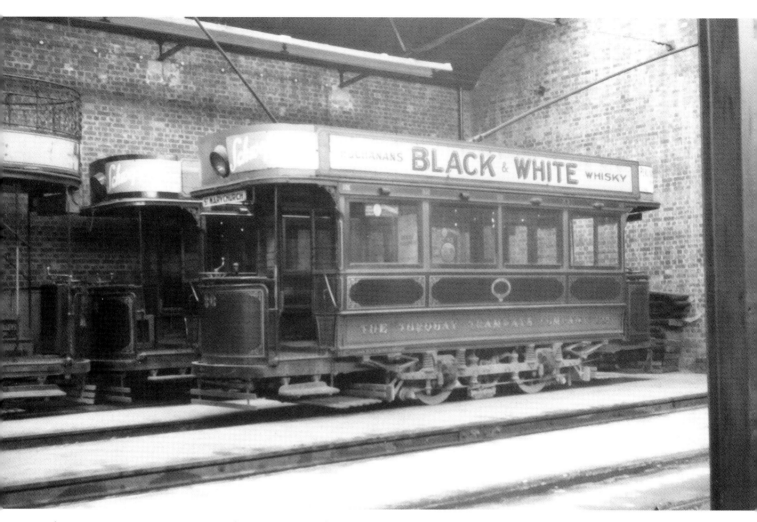

Above: **Between 21** August 1901 and 21 August 1921 the Taunton Electric Traction Co Ltd operated 3ft 6in gauge trams over a route that extended for slightly more than 1½ miles. The first batch of six trams were sold to Leamington & District in 1905 and, following the closure of the Taunton system in 1921, five of the second batch of six cars were sold for further service. Of these, three went to the Torquay Tramways Co Ltd, becoming the new owner's Nos 34-36. Two of these cars are seen in the operator's brown and yellow livery on 29 September 1930. The three cars were modified for one-man operation and were generally used on the route from St Marychurch to Torre station; this was to be converted with the bulk of the Torquay system – the exception being the Paignton route that succumbed earlier – on 31 January 1934. *Hugh Nicol/National Tramway Museum*

Opposite above: **In 1902,** the Middleton Electric Traction Co Ltd acquired four single-deck combination cars from Brush; these were numbered 22-25 and were mounted on Brush B type bogies. Two of the batch – Nos 24 and 25 – were sold for £240 each to another BET subsidiary – the Potteries Electric Traction Co Ltd – in 1916, with a third following in 1919, again for £240, with the final one following in 1920, this time for £250. The trams became Potteries Nos 99 (ii), 100 (ii), 119 and 120. Before they entered service in Stoke, all were re-gauged from standard gauge to 4ft 0in and were rebuilt as fully enclosed by replacing the transverse seating of the open central section with longitudinal seats and extending the bodywork over the open section. The quartet remained in service until the final conversion of the Potteries system in 1928. *Barry Cross Collection/Online Transport Archive*

Opposite below: **The second** batch of second-hand cars acquired by the Potteries Electric Traction Co Ltd were three single-deck cars acquired from Sheffield Corporation in October 1920. The three – Sheffield Nos 58, 96 and 97 – were all new in 1899; No 58 was built by ERT&CW whilst the other two were supplied by Brush. All were originally fitted with Brill 21E standard-gauge four-wheel trucks in Sheffield but these were replaced by 4ft 0in-gauge Peckham 10A four-wheel trucks before entering service in Stoke. Nos 96 and 97 became Nos 122/23 (although not necessarily in order) whilst No 58 became No 121 and this is illustrated here. No 122 was seriously damaged in an accident when it ran away on Hartshill Bank in 1922; it was never returned to service. The remaining two survived until the final abandonment of the Potteries system on 11 July 1928. *Barry Cross Collection/Online Transport Archive*

Above: In 1921, Liverpool Corporation sold the bodies of three trams – Nos 48-50 (originally Nos 479-81) – to the Tynemouth & District Electric Traction Co Ltd for £70 each. Presumably, the intention was to fit the bodies to replacement 3ft 6in gauge trucks for operation over the company route; in the event, however, the trio passed to the Gateshead & District Tramways Co where they were to become Nos 29 (ii), 30 (ii) and 38 (ii). The cars had originally been built at Liverpool's Lambeth Road works and were open-top and lacking canopies when received by Gateshead & District. Entering service in 1922 equipped with Brill 21E four-wheel trucks, the trams proved to be unpopular with the crews due to the lack of protection and, in 1925, all three were rebuilt with open-balcony top covers, enclosed lower-deck vestibules and altered staircases. This Second World War era view – evinced by the white painted fender and headlamp shield – of No 30 shows the type in its rebuilt form. The three cars were to remain in service until withdrawal in 1950. *Barry Cross Collection/Online Transport Archive*

Opposite: In 1921, the 3ft 6in Cheltenham & District Light Railway Co ordered four open-top double-deck cars from English Electric; fitted with Preston-built Peckham Pendulum four-wheel trucks, the quartet were to become Nos 21-24. However, prior to delivery, No 24 was diverted to another subsidiary of Balfour Beatty & Co – the Leamington & Warwick Electrical Co Ltd – where it entered service as No 14. The three-mile Leamington & Warwick was converted to bus operation on 16 August 1930; one of the company fleet – No 11 – was sold to the L&CBER (but did not enter service). Nos 9 and 14 were stored for a year pending a possible sale to the same operator (as were seven withdrawn Cheltenham & District cars); however, the L&CBER preferred to obtain single-deck cars – from Accrington – and both Nos 9 and 14 were subsequently scrapped. One of the ex-Cheltenham cars – No 21 – was rescued for preservation in 1960, having been used as a garden store since 1930, and was restored at Crich. The car is now owned by Cheltenham Borough Council. *D.W.K. Jones Collection/Online Transport Archive*

Two of the remaining three Taunton single-deck cars were sold to the Gravesend & Northfleet Electric Tramways where, after being converted to standard gauge, they entered service in 1921 as Nos 7 and 8, the second cars in the fleet to carry these numbers, replacing two of the fleet's existing bogie double-deck cars. No 7 was converted by its new owner into a one-man car and is pictured here in the depot at Northfleet. The Gravesend system was finally converted to bus operation on 28 February 1929. *Hugh Nicol/National Tramway Museum*

On 1 July 1921, the BET-owned Oldham, Ashton-under-Lyne & Hyde Electric Tramways Co Ltd ceased to operate, its service being replaced by those operated by Ashton-under-Lyne Corporation, Manchester Corporation and SHMD (on behalf of Hyde Corporation) with the company's fleet of trams dispersed between the three successor operators. Manchester Corporation acquired five of the fleet via Audenshaw UDC; four of these – Nos 14-17 – were Brush-built single-deck cars fitted with Peckham Cantilever four-wheel trucks. Never entering service with Manchester, this quartet was sold to Ayr Corporation in 1922 where they were to become Nos 25-28. No 27 is illustrated here heading south along Main Street towards the bridge across the River Ayr. The Ayr Corporation system was converted to bus operation on 31 December 1931. *Barry Cross Collection/Online Transport Archive*

In 1922, Gateshead & District acquired the bodies of eight Sheffield Corporation trams; these were Nos 16, 35, 37 and 38, all built by G.F. Milnes & Co, No 74 built by ER&TCW and Nos 176/82/86 manufactured by the Cravens Railway Carriage & Wagon Co of Darnall. All were new originally in 1899 or 1900, with the exception of the three Cravens-built cars that dated to 1902. Originally open-top and lacking platform canopies, all eight had short top covers fitted whilst in operation in Sheffield. The actual order of the renumbered cars is uncertain, but the three Cravens-built cars became Nos 31 (ii), 35 (ii) and 42 (ii) whilst the other five became Nos 24 (ii), 25 (ii), 33 (ii), 36 (ii) and 37 (ii). All were fitted with Brill 21E four-wheel trucks and entered service between October 1922 and May 1924; lower-deck vestibules and open-balcony top covers were added during rebuilding between December 1925 and June 1926. No 35 was withdrawn in 1947; the remainder survived until 1951 and here No 33 is seen at the Museum in Newcastle on 4 March 1950. The lower deck of No 33 was salvaged for preservation and has now been restored at the National Tramway Museum to the condition in which it operated as Sheffield No 74. *John Meredith/Online Transport Archive*

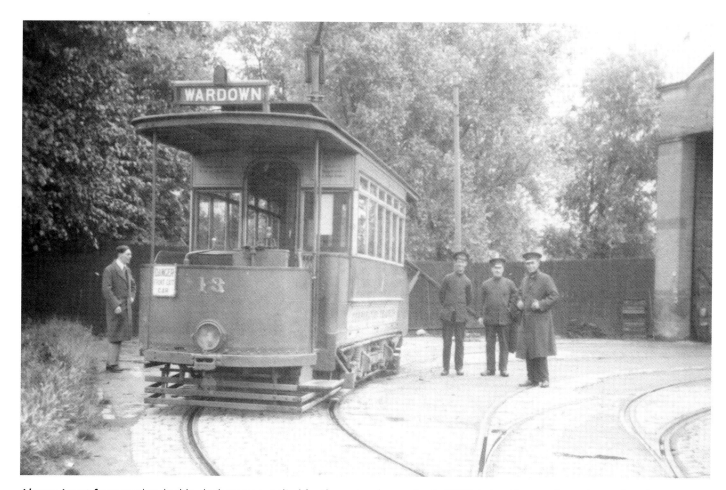

Above: **Apart from** twelve double-deck trams supplied for the system's opening in 1908, Luton Corporation only employed one other passenger tram; this was No 13, a single-deck car acquired from Glasgow Corporation. This tram had an interesting history in Glasgow; originally a horse tram dating from the 1890s, it was converted to an electric car fitted with a Brill 21E four-wheel truck before re-entering service in 1903. It was one of 120 horse trams converted by Glasgow Corporation between 1899 and 1903. No 118, withdrawn in May 1920, was one of the last to survive in service and, following withdrawal, it lost its upper-deck seats and was used on an experimental – and short-lived – parcels service. Its final work in Glasgow was as a ticket box car. Sold to Luton in May 1923, it was re-gauged from 4ft 7¾in to standard gauge before entering service; it operated primarily on the Wardown route and is seen here outside the corporation's depot off Park Street. The Luton system was converted to bus operation on 16 April 1932. *Barry Cross Collection/Online Transport Archive*

Opposite above: **Having acquired** three single-deck trams from Sheffield Corporation in 1918, five years later the Musselburgh & District Electric Light & Traction Co Ltd went back there to purchase three open-balcony double-deck four-wheel cars. The three Sheffield cars were Nos 141, which had originally been an open-top car when built by G.F. Milnes & Co in 1901, 170, also originally open-top when supplied by the Cravens Railway Carriage & Wagon Co Ltd in 1902, and 252, which was fitted with a top cover from new and had been built in the corporation's own workshops in 1905. The last named is seen in operation in Sheffield on Wolstenholme Road, Sheffield, on the Nether Edge service on a postcard franked on 24 September 1910. The three – which were to become Nos 20-22 in Scotland – were all fitted with Brill 21E four-wheel trucks whilst with Musselburgh & District. The final company's final operations occurred on 31 March 1928 when the last workmen's duties were run; regular services had ceased on 1 March of the same year. *Barry Cross Collection/Online Transport Archive*

Opposite below: **In 1920,** the Sunderland District Electric Tramways Ltd acquired eight new open-balcony cars from Brush; these were fitted with Brush-built 21E four-wheel trucks. The fleet numbers allocated are uncertain although it is believed that they were probably 35-38 plus four numbers reused from the earlier – 1905-built – cars that they replaced. Their life on Wearside was limited, being sold to Bolton Corporation in 1924 when the first section of the Sunderland District system was converted to bus operation. Becoming Bolton Nos 131-38, the ex-Sunderland cars were all withdrawn in 1933. Here, one of the type – No 133 – is seen on the extreme right alongside Bolton No 78; the latter was one of a batch of twenty-two cars supplied by ERT&CW in 1901 on Brill 22E bogies that were originally open-top. *John Meredith Collection/Online Transport Archive*

Wolstenholme Road, Sheffield

Above: **During the** early 1920s, Ipswich Corporation converted its 3ft 6in gauge tramway to trolleybus operation thus rendering its fleet of thirty-six open-top tramcars, all built by Brush in 1903 on Brush AA four-wheel trucks, surplus to requirements. In 1925, the Scarborough Tramways Co acquired five complete trams at £50 each plus the body of a sixth for £15. The latter, which was to become Scarborough No 21, was fitted with the Brush Conaty four-wheel truck that had originally been fitted to the first Scarborough No 21. The body of this car had been spectacularly written off when, while ascending the 1 in 10 gradient from Valley Road to Falconers Road on a service from South Sands to North Side, it lost adhesion and ran back down the hill before derailing and falling 30ft through the roof of the Aquarium ballroom. Although the driver was injured, there were fortunately no fatalities. Here one of the ex-Ipswich cars, No 24, is pictured on Foreshore Road in front of the Grand Picture House. The building, originally opened as the Grand Skating Rink, reopened as a cinema in 1914; damaged by German bombing on 16 December 1914 – one of the earliest aerial attacks on Britain during the First World War – the building was rebuilt and survived until final closure in the late 1940s. The ex-Ipswich cars survived until the final closure of the Scarborough system on 30 September 1931. *Barry Cross Collection/Online Transport Archive*

Opposite above: **In 1925,** Mansfield & District Light Railways, a subsidiary of the Midland Counties Electric Supply Co (itself a subsidiary of Balfour Beatty), borrowed three trams from another subsidiary – the Nottingham & Derbyshire Tramways Co Ltd – which became Nos 29-31. A shortage of trams on Notts & Derby led to No 29 being returned the following year, but the remaining two remained with Mansfield & District until its final closure on 9 October 1932; here, No 30 is pictured in Market Place, Mansfield in 1932, towards the end of the system's life. The three trams were all part of a batch of twelve – Nos 1-12 – which were supplied by UEC on Peckham P22 four-wheel trucks in 1913 for the opening of the Notts & Derby route; three – Nos 1-3 – were fitted with open-balcony top covers but the trio loaned to Mansfield & District remained open-top until withdrawal. *Maurice O'Connor/National Tramway Museum*

Opposite below: **In 1913,** Sunderland District Electric Tramways Ltd acquired sixteen new open-balcony double-deck cars from Brush; fitted with the same manufacturer's flexible four-wheel truck, the cars operated on Wearside until the company's route was converted to bus operation on 12 July 1925. Following this, the sixteen cars were sold to Grimsby Corporation – as Nos 41-56 (as illustrated here by No 52) – where they remained in operation until the last trams operated on 31 March 1937. *Maurice O'Connor/National Tramway Museum*

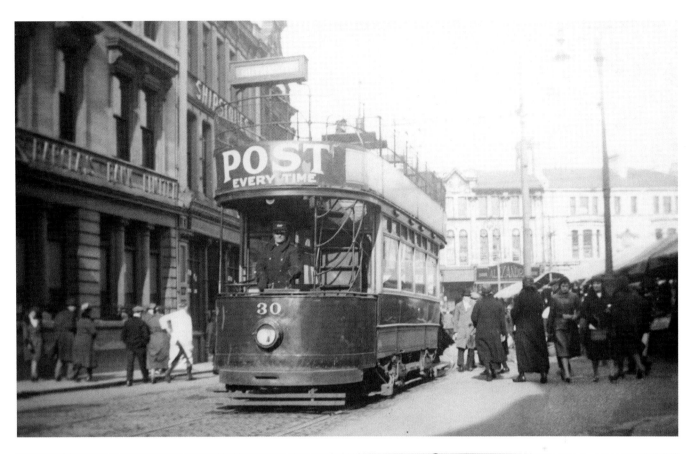

Above: **In 1903,** the Middleton Electric Traction Co Ltd in acquired eight single-deck trailer cars from another BET subsidiary, the Oldham, Ashton-under-Lyne & Hyde Electric Tramway Co, in exchange for four single-deck cars. Built by Brush on Peckham trucks and new in May 1900, the trams retained their original fleet numbers in Middleton as the company's existing tram fleet numbered up to No 26. The new owner converted the eight with new Dick Kerr-supplied motors and controllers; in 1909, Nos 28 and 34 received replacement Brush AA four-wheel trucks. In 1925, following the purchase of the company's assets by the councils of Chadderton, Middleton and Rochdale, Oldham Corporation acquired Chadderton's interests along with these eight single-deck cars. In Oldham's ownership, the eight became Nos 113-20 and here No 119 is seen on Middleton Road in 1927. The cars were to be re-trucked with Brill 21E four-wheel rucks in Oldham. The first to be withdrawn was No 119 in 1933, followed by No 117 in 1934; the remaining six cars were all withdrawn in 1935. *Barry Cross Collection/Online Transport Archive*

Opposite above: **Rochdale Corporation** also acquired trams from the Middleton Electric Traction Co Ltd in 1925. These were five open-top double-deck cars that were Nos 11 (ii) to 15 (ii) with the Middleton company. The quintet were built by Brush in 1905 on the same supplier's Conaty four-wheel trucks and had been acquired in place of five of the original combination cars that had been sold in that year. In Rochdale, they became Nos 2 (ii) and 12 (ii) to 15 (ii). All five were withdrawn by the end of 1931; the final Rochdale trams operated on 12 November 1932. *D.W.K. Jones Collection/Online Transport Archive*

Opposite below: **The final** operator to acquire trams from the Middleton Electric Traction Co Ltd in 1925 was Manchester Corporation, which acquired ten single-deck combination cars – Nos 1-10 – which had originally been delivered in 1901 on Brill 22E bogies. These were allocated fleet numbers 994-1003 by the corporation. Of the ten, No 994 entered service in 1925, Nos 995 – illustrated here – and 996 in 1926, No 997 (having been slightly modified) in 1927, No 998 in 1928 and No 999 in 1929. A seventh car was modified and re-entered service in 1928 as No 529 as a replacement for the original single-deck car with that number, which had been withdrawn. The corporation already operated a number of similar cars – Nos 512-36, 649-68 and 836-47 – primarily for use on the circular route 53. It was the decision to convert this service to bus operation progressively between 3 March 1930 to 6 April 1930 that resulted in the remaining three ex-Middleton cars not entering service and the conversion resulted in the withdrawal of the vast majority of the single-deck fleet. Of the ex-Middleton cars, all succumbed during 1930 with the exception of Nos 529, which was in use as a works car until late 1937, and No 997, which also survived until towards the end of the decade. *Barry Cross Collection/Online Transport Archive*

Above: **During 1921** and 1922, H. Orme White of the Great Grimsby Street Tramways Co designed and had built in the company's own workshops No 40; this unique tram – effectively the tramcar equivalent of the open charabanc – was known as the 'Tram Coach' and provided seating for forty passengers. Fitted with a second-hand Brill 21E truck – probably from 1903 ER&TCW-built No 30 – the car was used to provide round trips between Cleethorpes Kingsway and People's Park in Grimsby. The tram and service proved successful but, with the imminent transfer of the section of the company's system in Grimsby to the corporation – completed on 6 April 1925 – No 40 was re-gauged to 4ft 7¾in and transferred to the Portsdown & Horndean Tramway, another subsidiary of the Provincial Tramways Co Ltd, where it re-entered service as No 17. However, its length – 31ft with a 12ft 9in overhang at both ends – meant that it fouled the pavements in Portsmouth and, following complaints from the corporation, the car was withdrawn following one summer's use in Hampshire. *H. Orme White/via Barry Cross Collection/Online Transport Archive*

Opposite above: **In the** mid-1920s, Dover Corporation, in need of supplementing and replacing its existing fleet, acquired second-hand cars from a number of operators. The first two – destined to become Dover Nos 8 and 9 – were acquired from Darlington Corporation in 1926. The Darlington system ceased to operate on 10 April 1926, being replaced by trolleybuses, which rendered the two open-balcony cars supplied by UEC – Nos 17 and 18 – surplus to requirements. These cars were acquired by Dover for £250 apiece and, retaining their original Preston flexible four-wheel trucks, were allocated primarily to the Maxton route; here, No 8 is pictured at the Maxton terminus. Both of the ex-Darlington cars survived to the final conversion of the Dover system on 31 December 1936. *Hugh Nicol/National Tramway Museum*

Opposite below: **The second** batch of second-hand cars acquired by Dover Corporation were five open-top cars from West Hartlepool Corporation in 1927. Numbered 1-5 by West Hartlepool, the five trams were built by UEC and new in 1914; fitted with UEC-built Preston flexible four-wheel trucks, the cars retained their original fleet numbers in Dover. Although No 2 was to be repainted in the green livery that Dover had used, the remaining four – such as No 3 seen here at the Pier terminus – retained their original dark red and ivory livery. Following an agreement with East Kent, whereby the company-operated buses would replace the trams, the last Dover trams operated on 31 December 1936. The ex-West Hartlepool trams – along with the rest of the Dover fleet – were subsequently scrapped. *Hugh Nicol/National Tramway Museum*

Above: **In 1905,** for the opening of the line, the 3ft 6in gauge Burton & Ashby Light Railway acquired thirteen open-top cars from Brush fitted to the same manufacturer's AA four-wheel trucks; Nos 1-13 were supplemented by a further seven – Nos 14-20 – from the same builder the following year. Following the closure of the route on 19 February 1927, ten of the cars were acquired by the Tynemouth & District Electric Traction Co Ltd. Allocated the fleet numbers 22-31, only three – Nos 22-24 – actually entered service on Tyneside with Nos 23 and 24 being renumbered 1 and 6 respectively shortly after entering service. Pictured in Cullercoates during 1929 is No 22. The three cars were to remain in service until the final conversion of the Tynemouth & District route on 4 August 1931. One of the ex-Burton & Ashby cars – albeit not one of those transferred to Tyneside – survives in preservation; No 14 is currently based at Statfold Barn having been repatriated from the USA. *John Meredith Collection/Online Transport Archive*

Opposite above: **During 1903** and 1904, Wigan Corporation acquired a batch of eighteen single-deck cars – Nos 63-80 – from ER&TCW; in 1927, St Helens Corporation bought two of the batch – Nos 68 and 77 – at £350 each. Fitted with Brill 22E bogies, the two cars were initially Nos 30 (ii) and 31 (ii) with St Helens but were to be renumbered 13 (ii) and 14 (ii) in 1929 and it is this guise that the latter is recorded here. The two cars were finally withdrawn in 1935; the final St Helens trams operated on 31 March 1936. *Barry Cross Collection/Online Transport Archive*

Opposite below: **In late** 1928, Dover Corporation acquired two open-balcony cars from the Birmingham & Midland Joint Tramways Committee; these were Nos 15 and 17, which became Nos 11 and 12 on the South Coast. Both had originally been built at the committee's works at Tividale and were fitted with four-wheel trucks that were also manufactured at Tividale. Alongside these, the corporation also acquired three top covers from the committee; these were fitted to the corporation's Nos 22-27. Here, one of the two complete cars – No 12 – is recorded at Buckland, close to the depot, on the route out towards River on Lewisham Road. *Hugh Nicol/ National Tramway Museum*

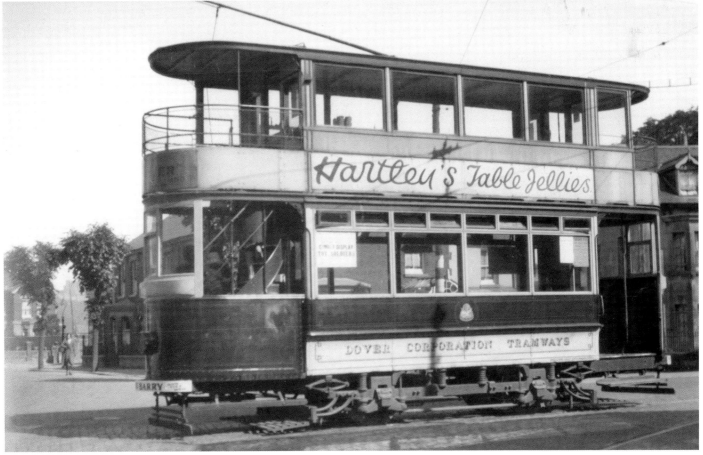

Above: **In 1921,** the BET-owned Worcester Electric Traction Co Ltd supplemented its existing fleet of fifteen 3ft 6in gauge open-top four-wheel cars through the acquisition of two new open-top cars – Nos 16 and 7 – that were built for the company by the Tividale Works of the associated Birmingham & Midland Tramways Joint Committee on Brill 21E four-wheel trucks. Towards the end of the decade, Worcester Corporation considered acquiring the tramway and converting it to trolleybus operation but an alternative solution – replacement by buses operated by the Birmingham & Midland Motor Omnibus Co Ltd (better known as Midland Red) – was agreed and the last Worcester trams operated on 31 May 1928. Nos 16 and 17 were acquired in 1928 by the Balfour Beatty-owned Cheltenham & District Light Railway Co, where they were renumbered 25 and 24 respectively. However, they were not to survive long in Gloucestershire as, the following year, Balfour Beatty proposed replacing the Cheltenham trams with trolleybuses. Although this plan did not proceed, buses replaced trams in two stages during 1930 with the last operated on 31 December of that year. Here, No 25 is seen standing inside the company's sole depot – St Mark's – alongside No 12, which was last of four open-top four-wheel cars supplied by the Gloucester Railway Carriage & Wagon Co Ltd in 1902 and which operated as a single-decker after 1920. *Charles F. Klapper/copyright The Bus Archive*

Opposite above: **Following the** final conversion of the Potteries Electric Traction Co Ltd's system on 11 July 1928, the Wemyss & District Tramways Co Ltd acquired No 82; this was one of a batch of fifteen single-deck cars – Nos 71-85 – that were built by the Shrewsbury-based Midland Railway Carriage & Wagon Co Ltd on Brill 22E maximum traction bogies in 1900. The tram had been extensively rebuilt by PET in 1924. Before entering service it was re-equipped with M&G equal wheel bogies – these were again possibly ex-PET re-gauged from 4ft 0in to 3ft 6in – and had platform vestibules built at the Wemyss depot at Aberhill. This car – illustrated here at the Leven terminus in 1931 – was to become Wemyss No 20. It survived until the closure of the system in January 1932. *Barry Cross Collection/Online Transport Archive*

Opposite below: **Later in** 1928, Wemyss & District Tramways Co Ltd acquired a second tram from PET. This was probably No 95, which was one of a batch of twenty cars – Nos 86-105 – supplied by Brush, again on Brill 22E bogies, during 1900 and 1901. Again fitted with replacement M&G bogies and platform vestibules, the car became No 21 in Fife and – pictured here in front of Aberhill depot – was also to survive until January 1932. *Barry Cross Collection/Online Transport Archive*

Above: **Following the** final conversion of the Jarrow & District Electric Tramways Co Ltd system on 30 June 1929, the company's two ex-Gravesend & District cars – Nos 5 and 6 – were sold to South Shields Corporation where they became Nos 48 and 29 respectively. Entering service in March 1930, the two cars – with their reversed Brill 22E maximum traction bogies – were used on the Cleadon Light Railway; however, a tendency to derail elsewhere on the system led to the bogies being switched to a more normal arrangement. Here, one of the two is seen outside the corporation's depot – on Dean Road – in original condition with reversed bogies. The two cars remained open-top and un-vestibuled through to withdrawal in 1935. *Hugh Nicol/National Tramway Museum*

Opposite above: **In 1919,** following the conversion of the corporation's small – 1½ route mile – network from the Griffiths-Bedall surface stud system to conventional overhead, Lincoln acquired three new open-balcony double-deck cars from English Electric on Brill 21E four-wheel trucks. Originally lacking enclosed lower-deck platforms, these were added during their years in Lincoln. A decade on from delivery, with the conversion of the system to bus operation, the three cars – Nos 9-11 – were sold to Preston Corporation in 1929 for £675 where they became Nos 13, 18 and 22. The first of the trio is illustrated here at the town centre terminus of route R awaiting departure for Ribbleton. The three cars were destined to have a short career in North Lancashire; the last Preston trams operated on 15 December 1935. *Barry Cross Collection/Online Transport Archive*

Opposite below: **Having acquired** two complete trams from the Birmingham & Midland Joint Tramways Committee, Dover Corporation acquired more equipment – this time from the scrap merchant A. Davey & Co Ltd who was dismantling the committee's fleet – in 1930. In all, five open-balcony bodies and trucks were acquired along with other equipment. These were used to construct five cars – Nos 6, 7, 10, 14 and 17 – by the corporation; unfortunately, the original committee fleet numbers are unrecorded but four of the five were built originally by Brush in 1914 and rebuilt at Tividale in 1915. The one exception – Dover No 14 – was a further example of the batch built at Tividale in 1915 and was similar to Dover Nos 11 and 12; this car is pictured here in 1932 in the dark red and ivory livery adopted by the corporation after the purchase of the five trams from West Hartlepool. *Maurice O'Connor/National Tramway Museum*

FULFORD TRAM TERMINUS.

Above: In 1920, Burton-on-Trent Corporation increased its relatively small fleet through the purchase of four open-balcony cars from English Electric. Fitted with Preston 21E four-wheel trucks, the cars – Nos 21-24 – were to survive in the East Midlands until the final conversion of the Burton system to bus operation on 31 December 1929. In February 1930, York Corporation acquired the four cars at £152 each but, before they were transferred to Yorkshire, the quartet were converted into open-top form using trolleypoles and standards reused from withdrawn open-top Burton trams. The four cars became York Nos 42-45. By this date, however, consideration as to the future of the corporation's transport department was under consideration and, following an agreement to set up a joint undertaking with the West Yorkshire Road Car Co, the last trams operated on 16 November 1935. Here, No 43 is pictured at the Fulford terminus. *Barry Cross Collection/Online Transport Archive*

Opposite above: For the opening of the Tyneside Tramways & Tramroads Co on 22 September 1902 G.F. Milnes & Co supplied eighteen open-top trams; of these Nos 1-4 were fitted with Brill 27G bogies, whilst the remainder had Brill 21E four-wheel trucks. In 1930, following the final conversion of the company's system on 6 April of that year, South Shields Corporation acquired for a total of £500 two of the bogie cars – Nos 3 and 4 – which became Nos 46 and 47. This view records No 46 between then and 1933 when the car was converted into a single-decker through the removal of the stairs and upper-deck seating. It remained in this condition, with extra seating provided on the platforms, until 1937 when it and No 47, which remained in open-top condition throughout its career, were both withdrawn. *Maurice O'Connor/National Tramway Museum*

Opposite below: During 1929 and 1930, the 3ft 6in Merthyr Electric Traction & Lighting Co Ltd acquired the bodies of nine trams from the Birmingham & Midlands Tramways Joint Committee. These had all been constructed originally by the committee at its Tividale Works between 1913 and 1916 as balcony-top four-wheel cars. The original fleet numbers are unknown but they were to become Merthyr Nos 2, 7-9, 11, 13-16. Although constructed with balcony-top covers, the gradients of the Merthyr system required them to be converted into open-top form before entering service; they were also fitted with Brill 21E four-wheel trucks salvaged from the trams that they replaced. Six of the cars were fitted by committee curved lower-deck vestibule screens; the remaining three – Nos 7, 9 and 11 – had the committee's temporary screen when received in Wales. These were modified in Merthyr. Here three of the batch – Nos 7, 9 and 11 – are seen alongside ex-Birmingham Corporation No 6 at the system's one depot at Penydarren. The ex-committee cars survived until the final closure of the system on 23 August 1939. *W.A. Camwell/National Tramway Museum*

Above: Following the conversion of the 4ft 7¾in Gosport & Fareham Tramway, owned by the Portsmouth Street Tramways Co, to bus operation on 31 December 1929, seven of the fleet were transferred to the Portsdown & Horndean Tramway, owned by the Hampshire Light Railways (Electric) Co Ltd. This company, which (like the Gosport & Fareham) was a subsidiary of the Provincial Tramways Co Ltd, operated a six-mile route from Cosham to Horndean (extended south over Portsmouth Corporation track for a further 5½ miles in 1927). Nos 2, 8, 10, 14, 20-22 were transferred; Nos 2, 8 and 10 were originally built by Brush on the same supplier's 21E four-wheel trucks in 1905; these were to become Portsdown & Horndean Nos 2, 8 and 17 respectively. The remaining quartet was built by Milnes Voss on M&G 21EM four-wheel trucks in 1906; Nos 20-21 retained their original fleet numbers but No 14 was to become Portsdown & Horndean No 10 and No 22 was to become No 14. Portsdown & Horndean Nos 2, 10, 14 and 17 received replacement BEC SB60 four-wheel trucks from withdrawn trams whilst No 8 later received a M&G 21EM four-wheel truck; Nos 20 and 21 retained their original 21EM trucks. Portsdown & Horndean No 21 – ex-Gosport & Fareham No 21 – is recorded here. All seven survived until the conversion of the route to bus operation on 9 January 1935. *Barry Cross Collection/Online Transport Archive*

Opposite above: Of the remaining fifteen cars in the Gosport & Fareham fleet, twelve were transferred to the Great Grimsby Street Tramways Co, another subsidiary of the Provincial Tramways Co Ltd, also in 1930. These were to become Nos 1-3 (ii) and 22-30 (ii) on Humberside. Between 1931 and 1933, four of the batch – Nos 2, 3, 27 and 30 – were fitted with open-balcony top covers. All twelve were to pass to Cleethorpes UDC when the company's assets were transferred on 15 July 1936 and were to survive through to the final conversion of the ex-Great Grimsby system in July 1937. On 25 June 1933, No 22 is pictured with No 39; the latter was an open-top car constructed by the company itself in 1925. This too passed to Cleethorpes UDC in 1936 and was withdrawn the following year. *Maurice O'Connor/National Tramway Museum*

Opposite below: In 1930, the Llandudno & Colwyn Bay Electric Railway acquired its first second-hand tram; this was a car – generally believed to be No 11 – from the Leamington & Warwick Electrical Co Ltd, a company that had ceased to operate trams on 16 August 1930. No 11 had originally been supplied to the Taunton & West Somerset Electric Railways & Tramways Co Ltd in 1901 as part of a batch of six – Nos 1-6 – supplied by Brush on the same manufacturer's Type A four-wheel truck. No 11 was cut-down to single deck, albeit retaining its staircases, and used as a works car by the Leamington & Warwick company. Following its sale to the Llandudno & Colwyn Bay, it became No 23. It was to remain in service in North Wales until 1936, when it was replaced by a new No 23 – acquired second-hand from Bournemouth (see page 102) – although its body was to survive for a number of years in use as a shed. *H.B. Priestley/National Tramway Museum*

***Above*: In 1931,** Sunderland Corporation acquired two fully-enclosed lowbridge double-deck trams from Accrington Corporation. The two cars had been new in 1926 and had been built by Brush on Peckham PB four-wheel trucks. These were the last new trams acquired by Accrington and had to be re-gauged from 4ft 0in to standard gauge before operation in Sunderland. Originally Accrington Nos 42 and 43, they were to become Nos 19 and 20 on Wearside. Apart from re-gauging, the two trams were also to be re-motored – in 1938 – when they received 57hp English Electric motors. No 19 was to be scrapped in early 1953 whilst No 20 was to succumb in June of the same year. In this view, No 20 is pictured on Ryhope Road with a service towards Grangetown on 28 June 1952. This route was converted to bus operation on 30 November 1952. *John Meredith/Online Transport Archive*

***Opposite above*: In 1929** – with a view to an extension (never completed) from Pinhoe Road to Whipton – Exeter Corporation acquired four new open-top double-deck cars from Brush. Nos 1-4 (ii), fitted with Peckham P35 four-wheel trucks, were not to survive long in the West Country as a change of policy resulted in the conversion of the Exeter system to bus operation, with the last trams operating on 19 August 1931. No 3 is pictured here during its relatively short life in Devon. *Barry Cross Collection/Online Transport Archive*

***Opposite below*: Following the** conversion of the Exeter Corporation system, Halifax Corporation acquired the four cars delivered in 1929 for £200 apiece and renumbered them 128-131 – as illustrated by the first of the batch. The quartet, which remained open-top until closure, were used exclusively on the Triangle/Sowerby Bridge service; following conversion of this service to bus operation on 29 November 1938 – with No 129 being the last car to Sowerby Bridge – all four were withdrawn. *W.A. Camwell/Online Transport Archive*

Above: **Another purchaser** of Exeter's redundant trams in 1931 was closer to hand; Plymouth Corporation acquired nine cars –
Nos 26-34 – that had originally been built by Brush between 1921 and 1926. All of these, with the exception of Nos 26 and 27 (which
were fitted with Peckham P22 four-wheel trucks), were equipped with Brill 21E trucks. The Brill cars became Plymouth Nos 1-7, whilst
the two Peckham examples became Nos 8 and 9; one of the latter two is seen here. All of the nine cars were withdrawn by the end
of 1938 as the Plymouth system contracted although two of the batch – Nos 2 and 6 – were physically to survive until a number of
withdrawn trams were scrapped in 1942. *Barry Cross Collection/Online Transport Archive*

Opposite: **On 15** May 1931, the 3ft 6in gauge Kirkcaldy Corporation tramway operated for the last time, making redundant twenty-six
double-deck passenger trams. Although it had already been agreed that the Weymss & District was to be converted to bus operation,
no fewer than eight of the withdrawn Kirkcaldy cars were acquired. These were Kirkcaldy Nos 23-26 – which were the last new trams
acquired by the corporation in 1916 and were supplied by Hurst Nelson on the same manufacturer's solid-forged four-wheel trucks –
plus four from the earlier twenty-two cars; these had all been supplied by G.F. Milnes & Co between 1902 and 1904 and were fitted
with the same supplier's pressed steel four wheel trucks. Before the eight cars could operate on the Wemyss & District system, all
had to be converted to single-deck – a Board of Trade regulation – whilst platform vestibules were also constructed. Given that the
system was scheduled for conversion, the expenditure involved seems excessive given that the first four entered service in July 1931
and the final four in October – less than four months before the final conversion on 30 January 1932. Alan Brotchie posits that the
increased capacity that the new cars offered was to influence the issue of the replacement bus licences. This view of No 28 shows the
considerable work undertaken to make the octet suitable for operation and must date to that brief period when the car was in service.
Barry Cross Collection/Online Transport Archive

Above: In 1932, South Shields Corporation acquired two trams – Nos 29 and 30 – from Ayr Corporation; these had originally been supplied to Dumbarton Burgh & County Tramways – and were to become No 54 and 57 on Tyneside. Fitted with Peckham P22 four-wheel trucks, South Shields replaced these with 21E-type trucks supplied by Hurst Nelson. The two cars were renumbered 16 (ii) and 34 (ii) in 1934; the same year saw No 16 rebuilt as fully enclosed and it is in this guise that the tram is seen in front of the Lifeboat Memorial at the Pier Head terminus on Ocean Road; this section was converted to trolleybus operation on 11 April 1938. No 16 was one of the fleet that survived through to the final abandonment of the tramway network in South Shields on 31 March 1946. No 34 was not rebuilt and was withdrawn by 1939. *Barry Cross Collection/Online Transport Archive*

Opposite above: In 1915, Accrington Corporation acquired three-single deck cars – Nos 28-30 – from Brush; these were followed in 1920 by a further two – Nos 31 and 32. All were fitted from new with Brush MET type bogies. This is a manufacturer's photograph of the first of the quintet. *D.W.K. Jones Collection/Online Transport Archive*

Opposite below: Following the final closure of the 4ft 0in gauge Accrington Corporation system on 6 January 1932, the Llandudno & Colwyn Bay Electric Railway acquired five redundant single-deck cars – Nos 28-32. All had originally been fitted with Brush-built MET-type bogies although L&CBER Nos 1, 3 and 4 – ex-Accrington Nos 28, 30 and 31 – were sold without bogies and received M&G equal-wheel bogies from withdrawn L&CBER original Nos 1-5 of 1907. Nos 2 and 5 retained their original bogies, which had to be re-gauged to 3ft 6in before operation in North Wales. All five were scrapped following the closure of the L&CBER on 24 March 1956. Pictured on the single-track section along Gloddaeth Avenue in the early summer of 1954 is L&CBER No 4. *Phil Tatt/Online Transport Archive*

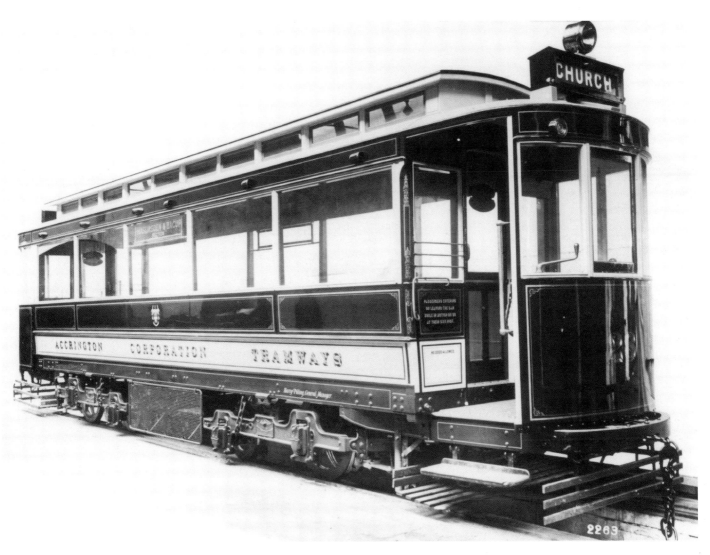

Above: In 1925, the Wemyss & District Tramways Co Ltd acquired its last wholly new tramcars; these were two single-deck cars – Nos 18 and 19 – supplied by Brush on the same manufacturer's maximum traction bogies. The final conversion of the 3ft 6in gauge system on 30 January 1932 rendered these two cars redundant and, as a result, they were acquired by the neighbouring Dunfermline & District Tramways Co, where they were to become Nos 45 and 44 respectively. This view records one of the cars outside the Dunfermline & District depot in Cowdenbeath. The straggling Dunfermline & District system – almost 18½ route miles in all – was finally converted to bus operation on 4 July 1937. *Barry Cross Collection/Online Transport Archive*

Opposite above: Following the disastrous fire at its Castleford depot in 1917, Yorkshire (West Riding) initially borrowed, and then bought, trams from Leeds Corporation; in 1920, the company acquired its last new trams – eight open-balcony cars supplied by English Electric on Preston Brill 21E four-wheel trucks. These were Nos 28, 31, 34, 35 and 37 plus three from Nos 23-25, 29, 33, 36 or 38. With the final conversion of the Yorkshire (West Riding) system on 25 July 1932, South Shields Corporation acquired two bodies – at £55 apiece – and, combined with second-hand trucks bought from Lanarkshire Tramways and motors from the LCC, created two trams – Nos 18 (ii) and 20 (ii) – as illustrated by this view of No 20 outside the corporation's Dean Road depot. The two cars were withdrawn by 1939. *Barry Cross Collection/Online Transport Archive*

Opposite below: In 1932, South Shields acquired six ex-Wigan Corporation open-balcony trams; new originally in 1914 as Nos 1-6 and built by UEC on Brill 43E1 bogies, the trams were purchased for £100 each, including delivery, from the scrap merchants who had bought the redundant trams following the final conversion of the Wigan system on 28 March 1931. Two of the six – ex-Wigan Nos 3 and 5 – were dismantled for spares and scrapped in 1934 whilst the remaining four – rebuilt as fully enclosed – entered service in South Shields between March 1933 and 1935 as Nos 23 (ii) (ex-Wigan No 4), 50 (ex-No 6), 51 (ex-No 1) and 52 (ex-No 2). No 52 was renumbered 33 (ii) in 1935 with its original number being taken by the new Brush-built car new in 1936. Of the four, three were withdrawn in 1943 leaving the survivor – No 23 (ii) – in service until the final conversion of the Ridgeway route on 1 April 1946. Here, No 50 is pictured at the Ridgeway terminus prior to heading northwards to the town terminus on Moon Street. *W.A. Camwell/National Tramway Museum*

Above: The last new trams acquired by Mansfield & District – in 1925 – were two fully-enclosed trams – Nos 27 and 28 – supplied by English Electric on Peckham P22 four-wheel trucks. Following the closure of the system on 9 October 1932, Sunderland Corporation acquired the two bodies and used them as the basis of two trams constructed on Wearside – Nos 21 and 24 – which were fitted with EMB lightweight four-wheel trucks and entered service in 1933. No 21 is seen at the terminus of the Durham Road route in the spring of 1952. This car was to be withdrawn in June 1953 but No 24 was to survive until the final closure of the Sunderland system in October 1954. *Phil Tatt/Online Transport Archive*

Opposite above: The last wholly new electric tramway to be opened in England was the short-lived Dearne District Light Railways, which opened on 14 July 1924 and was to survive less than a decade before conversion to bus operation on 30 September 1933. In order to operate the tramway, English Electric supplied thirty single-deck cars – Nos 1-30 – in two batches during 1923 and 1924 on Peckham P22 four-wheel trucks. One of the first batch of twenty-five – Nos 1-25 – supplied during 1923 and 1924 for the line's opening is pictured in Doncaster Road, Barnsley. Despite the proximity to the network of the Barnsley & District Electric Traction Co, the track of which is visible in the foreground, there was no physical track connection between the two. *Barry Cross Collection/Online Transport Archive*

Opposite below: Less than ten years old when the Dearne District Light Railways closed on 30 September 1933, four of the cars were acquired by Lytham St Annes Corporation in 1933 where they became Nos 51-54; No 52 is seen here. The quartet cost £125 each and were bought primarily for winter use on the through service to Gynn Square. However, the then manager of Blackpool – Walter Luff – disliked them and from the spring of 1934 they were used mainly on services within Lytham St Annes. All four were scrapped following the final withdrawal of the Lytham trams. *Barry Cross Collection/Online Transport Archive*

Above: **Another operator** to acquire redundant trams from Dearne District Light Railways was the Falkirk & District Tramways Co, which acquired five of the cars in 1933. The cars were modified before entry to service in 1934 by being slightly shortened and were re-gauged from 4ft 8½in to 4ft 0in. The five cars were destined to have only a short career in Scotland as the Falkirk system was converted to bus operation on 21 July 1936. In Falkirk the cars were numbered 11, 12 and 17-19 and here No 12 is pictured outside the company's sole depot on Larbert Road between Camelon and Larbert. In addition to the sale of the trams to Lytham St Annes and to Falkirk, the trucks and electrical equipment of the remaining twenty-one cars in the Dearne District fleet were also sold, this time to Hull Corporation. *Hugh Nicol/National Tramway Museum*

Opposite above: **Following the** final abandonment of the Accrington system in 1932, four fully-enclosed trams – Nos 38-41 – remained and one of these – No 39 – was sold to Lytham St Annes Corporation the following year. Becoming No 55 on the Fylde Coast, the tram was re-gauged from 4ft 0in to standard gauge before entering service. Accrington retained the remaining three cars – which had all been built originally by Brush in 1915 (Nos 38 and 39) and 1920 (Nos 40 and 41) on Brush-built MET-style bogies – in the expectation, never fulfilled, that Lytham St Annes might acquire them as well. Unlike Blackpool, which underwent significant modernisation during the 1930s, the trams in Lytham St Annes were destined to be converted to bus operation on 28 April 1937 with No 55 being scrapped thereafter. *D.W.K. Jones Collection/Online Transport Archive*

Opposite below: **The final** second-hand trams acquired by Dover Corporation came from Birmingham Corporation, via scrap dealers, in 1933. The purchase comprised two complete cars and two spare bodies; the latter – believed to be Dover Nos 19 and 20 – were fitted with Brill 21E four-wheel trucks reused from withdrawn cars. The four trams were originally constructed by UEC on Brill 21E trucks as open-top cars in 1905 but all had received open-balcony top covers by 1925. No 22 – as pictured here in 1934 at the Pier terminus – was reconverted to open-top condition by Dover with equipment salvaged from the original No 22 as it was required for use on the River route where the Board of Trade restrictions required the operation of open-top cars given the narrow gauge – 3ft 6in – of the Dover system. *Barry Cross Collection/Online Transport Archive*

Above: **Another operator** to acquire ex-Birmingham Corporation trams via the scrap dealer in 1933 was Merthyr Electric Traction & Lighting Co Ltd. which acquired four cars that became Nos 3 (ii), 4 (ii), 6 (ii),12 (ii) in South Wales. Three of the four were from the same batch of 1905-built cars that Dover acquired; the fourth, also a produce of UEC on Brill 21E truck, was ex-Birmingham No 226 that became Merthyr Tydfil No 12 and it is this car recorded here on 28 August 1938 – less than a year before the system was converted to bus operation on 23 August 1939 at Pontmorlais Circus, the triangular junction at heart of the Merthyr Tydfil system. Although the Birmingham trams had been fitted with open-balcony top covers, these were removed prior to operation in Wales. *W.A.Camwell/National Tramway Museum*

Opposite above: **Following the** demise of the 4ft 0in gauge system operated by Rawtenstall Corporation on 7 April 1932 – the date of the official last run; normal passenger services had ceased on 31 March 1932 – the scrap dealer A. Devey & Co Ltd sold a number of bodies to neighbouring Darwen Corporation. In 1933, Darwen constructed a new fully-enclosed double-deck based around the lower deck of the original No 10 – one of a batch of five open-top cars supplied by G.F. Milnes & Co on Brill 22E bogies in 1901 – combined with an ex-Rawtenstall top cover. In its rebuilt form, No 10 (ii) is seen here in front of the Darwen branch of F.W. Woolworth in Market Street. The shop was itself a relatively recent addition to the street; the building was completed in 1930. No 10 was withdrawn in 1940. Two other Darwen trams – Nos 9 (ii) and 11 (ii) – also incorporated elements acquired from Rawtenstall. The former was a fully enclosed car that was derived from a complete car whilst No 11 was an open-balcony car fitted to the Brill 21E four-wheel truck of the original No 11 (dating to 1901). *W.A. Camwell/National Tramway Museum*

Opposite below: **The last** new trams acquired by the South Lancashire Tramways Co were two open-balcony cars – Nos 44 (ii) and 45 (ii) – which were supplied English Electric on EMB Burnley bogies in 1927. However, the company, despite renewing its lease to operate the tramways that it had inherited from Farnworth UDC the same year, was soon to adopt a policy of converting its tram system to trolleybus operation. As a result, the last trams operated on 16 December 1933, although the Farnworth route – which had been operated by Bolton Corporation from the late 1920s on behalf of the company – was to survive until 12 November 1944. Taking advantage of the company closure, Bolton acquired two batches of trams from the company. Nos 44 and 45 were to become corporation Nos 33 (ii) and 34 (ii), with the latter illustrated here having been renumbered 334 in 1940. Both were withdrawn by the date of the final conversion in Bolton during March 1947. *Barry Cross Collection/Online Transport Archive*

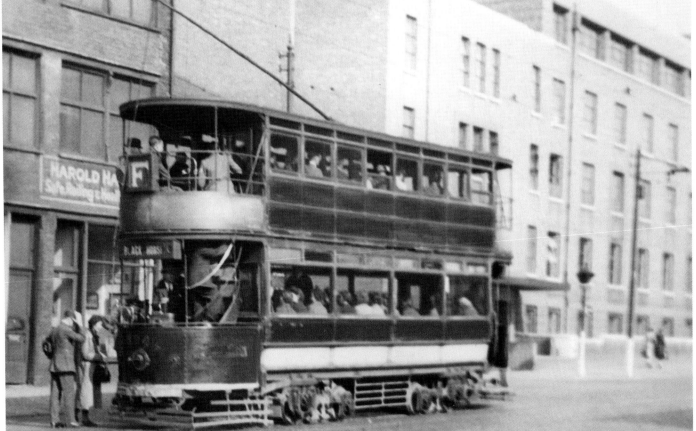

Above: **The second** group of trams acquired in December 1933 by Bolton Corporation from the South Lancashire Tramways Co were six older bogie cars that were part of a batch acquired by the company from Farnworth Council Tramways in 1906. These had originally been built by G.F. Milnes & Co and were new in 1901 and 1902; they were numbered 1-13 originally and Nos 46-58 by SLT. Fitted with Brill 22E maximum traction bogies, some of the thirteen cars were fitted with replacement English Electric open-balcony bodies between 1923 and 1926. The six cars sold to Bolton were Nos 47, 48, 50, 54, 55 and 58; these were to become Nos 35-40 and, following renumbering in 1940, Nos 333-40 and it is in this guise that No 339 is recorded here. All were withdrawn by the date of the final conversion of the Bolton system on 29 March 1947. *Barry Cross Collection/Online Transport Archive*

Opposite above: **With Lytham** St Annes having declined to purchase the remaining three Accrington fully-enclosed bogie cars, they were acquired in 1934 by Southend-on-Sea Corporation. Re-gauged to 3ft 6in, the trio – now renumbered 66-68 – survived until the final conversion of the system on 8 April 1942. No 66 – seen here as its trolleypole is turned – was originally Accrington No 38. *Barry Cross Collection/Online Transport Archive*

Opposite below: **Following the** demise of the network operated by the Torquay Tramways Co Ltd on 31 January 1934, Plymouth Corporation acquired twelve of the redundant cars despite the fact that the first conversions in Plymouth had already taken place. Torquay Nos 37-42 were six open-top cars supplied by Brush in 1923 (Nos 37 and 38), 1925 (Nos 39 and 40) and 1928 (Nos 41 and 42); all were fitted with the same manufacturer's maximum traction bogies and became Plymouth Nos 10-15 (ii; not in sequence). With the rapid contraction of the Plymouth system in the 1930s, the six cars were taken out of service in 1938 but not scrapped until four years later. This undated view of No 14 sees the tram awaiting departure from Drake Circus with a service towards Prince Rock; this route to be converted to bus operation on 23 February 1936. *Barry Cross Collection/Online Transport Archive*

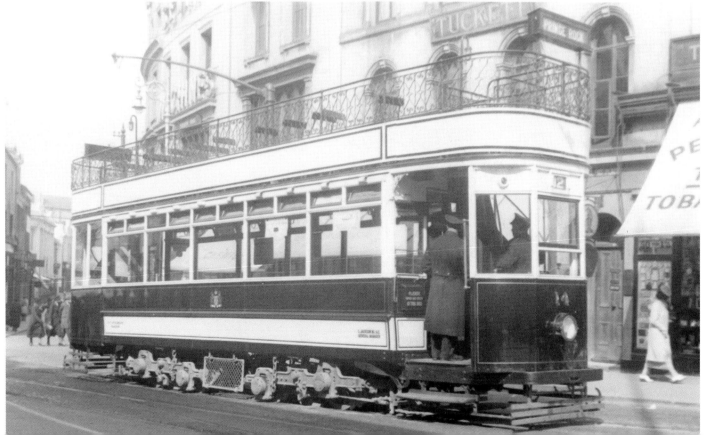

A second batch of ex-Torquay cars acquired by Plymouth were the latter's Nos 16-21 (ii). These had originally been amongst the first batch of open-top cars – Nos 1-18 – supplied by Brush during 1906 and 1907 for the opening of the Torquay system and had initially been fitted to operate using the Dolter stud system. When new, the trams were fitted with M&G radial trucks but seven of the batch – Nos 1, 7, 9, 10, 16-18 – received replacement Brill 21E four-wheel trucks during the 1920s. Of these six – the exception being No 1 – all were sold to Plymouth in 1934. Plymouth No 18 is seen alongside No 104; the latter was one of twelve cars – Nos 94-105 – supplied new to the corporation in 1930 by Brush. *Barry Cross Collection/Online Transport Archive*

The last wholly new trams acquired by Preston Corporation were three fully-enclosed cars built by the corporation itself on Preston Standard four-wheel trucks. Nos 30 (ii), 40 (ii) and 42 (ii) were new in 1928 and 1929 but were destined for only a short life in their home town; with buses replacing trams, No 42 was sold to Lytham St Annes in late 1934 where it was to become No 56. The last Preston trams operated on 15 December 1935. The career of No 56 on the Fylde Coast was fated to be even shorter than its life in Preston; it was withdrawn following the final conversion of the Lytham St Annes system on 28 April 1937. *John Meredith Collection/Online Transport Archive*

Following its acquisition of the sections of the Imperial Tramways Co Ltd within its boundaries on 3 April 1921, Middlesbrough Corporation initially undertook some fleet modernisation through the purchase of a bath of nine open-balcony cars – Nos 132-40 – from Hurst Nelson fitted with the same manufacturer's 22E bogies. New in 1921, the 3ft 7in gauge cars were barely a decade old when the last Middlesbrough trams operated on 9 June 1934. Four of the batch were sold for further service with Southend-on-Sea Corporation, where, after being re-gauged to 3ft 6in, they became Nos 62-65. No 63 is seen here heading east with a service on the circular route via Thorpe Bay. This car, along with Nos 62 and 64, were all withdrawn in 1939, leaving No 65 to soldier on until the final conversion of the Southend system – albeit not in service – on 8 April 1942. *W.A. Camwell/National Tramway Museum*

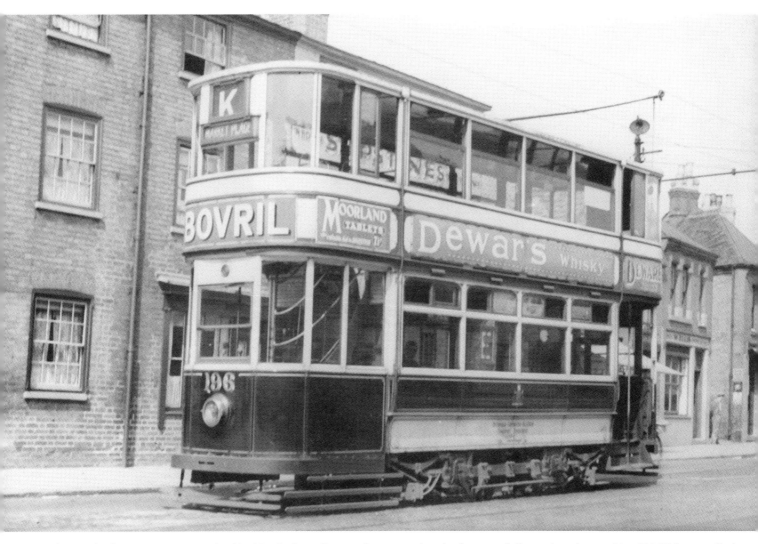

***Above*: The last** new trams acquired by Nottingham Corporation were a batch of twenty fully-enclosed cars – Nos 181-200 – supplied by English Electric on Peckham P22 four-wheel trucks during 1926 and 1927. By this stage, Nottingham was already contemplating the introduction of trolleybuses – the first route was introduced on 10 April 1927 – and the decision was made to abandon the tramway system. One of the batch – No 196 – is seen at the Arnold terminus in June 1935. Of the twenty cars, nineteen were sold to Aberdeen Corporation. *D.W.K. Jones Collection/Online Transport Archive*

***Opposite above*: Following the** final closure of the Nottingham system on 5 September 1936, Aberdeen Corporation acquired eighteen of the trams (Nos 181-94/96-99; a nineteenth car – No 195 – was acquired as a source of spare parts); these became Nos 1 (ii) to 18 (ii) and No 10 is seen on Castle Street as the driver changes the point on 24 January 1949. Nos 12, 14 and 18 were fitted with Brill 21E four-wheel truck for operation in Aberdeen; the remainder retained their P22 trucks. The purchase of twenty new streamlined bogie cars – Nos 19-38 – resulted in the withdrawal of all of the ex-Nottingham cars between 1949 and 1951. *Michael H. Waller*

***Opposite below*: In 1930,** Portsmouth Corporation constructed, in its own workshops on a Peckham cantilever four-wheel truck, a fully-enclosed tram. No 1 was, unfortunately, destined to be a one-off as the process of tramway conversion commenced the following year and the last trams operated on the 4ft 7¾in gauge system on 10 November 1936. The six-year old tram was sold to Sunderland Corporation where it was initially No 52. The original truck was replaced in 1938 by an EMB truck reused from Sunderland No 32. As a result of the construction of a new streamlined tram – No 52 – the last new tram acquired by the corporation, No 52 was renumbered as 45 in 1940. It is in this guise that the car is pictured here at the Seaburn terminus in April 1952; it was to be withdrawn early in the following year. *Phil Tatt/Online Transport Archive*

Above: **Between 1914** and 1924, the 3ft 6in gauge tramway operated by Bournemouth Corporation acquired fifty open-top bogie cars. Nos 83-92 were supplied by UEC in 1914 whilst Nos 93-112 and Nos 113-32 came from Brush in 1921 and between 1924 and 1926 respectively. All were fitted with Brill 22E maximum traction bogies. The UEC-built cars were delivered with open-lower deck platforms; these were, however, to be enclosed whilst the Brush-built examples had enclosed lower-deck platforms from new. In the early 1930s the corporation decided on a policy of tramcar replacement and the last trams were operated on 8 April 1936. No 121, pictured here operating on a service towards Poole, was one of 10 trams sold to the Llandudno & Colwyn Bay Electric Railway; it became No 8 in the North Wales fleet. *Barry Cross Collection/Online Transport Archive*

Opposite above: **In 1936,** the L&CBER took advantage of the abandonment of the 3ft 6in gauge tramway operated by Bournemouth Corporation to acquire ten double-deck passenger trams. Although powers to operate double-deck cars had – with restrictions – been obtained in 1916, these were the first non-single-deck cars to be owned by the company. On 30 September 1951, No 7 is pictured at the Colwyn Bay terminus prior to heading back towards Llandudno. This had originally been Bournemouth No 116 and was one of a batch. Of the ten cars bought by the company, five were from the batch constructed between 1924 and 1926, four were from the batch of similar cars delivered in 1921 and one – No 6 – was from the UEC-built batch that were new in 1914. As L&CBER No 6, the car was preserved on withdrawal in 1955 and is now on display at Crich having been restored as Bournemouth No 85. The remaining nine cars were all withdrawn following the conversion of the line on 24 March 1956 and scrapped. More recently, another ex-Bournemouth body – No 86 – has been rescued and cosmetically restored as a further L&CBER car by the Llandudno & Colwyn Bay Tramway Society, an organisation that also owns another – unrestored – Bournemouth body (No 101). *Julian Thompson/Online Transport Archive*

Opposite below: **Alongside the** ten passenger cars that the L&CBER acquired from Bournemouth Corporation in 1936, the company also bought the corporation's rail grinder. This was to become No 23 on the L&CBER initially; it was renumbered 23A in 1946 following the purchase of the two ex-Darwen Corporation cars and is seen in this condition in the company's Rhos-on-Sea depot on 22 July 1951. The car had originally one of four cars – Nos 1-4 – that were built for the Poole & District Electric Tramways Co Ltd in 1901 by G.F. Milnes & Co on a Brill 21E four-wheel truck, the car had become Bournemouth No 55 on the corporation's take-over of the company's operations in 1905. It was converted into a rail grinder in 1921. Surviving until the end of the L&CBER in March 1956, No 23A was subsequently scrapped. *Ian L. Wright/Online Transport Archive*

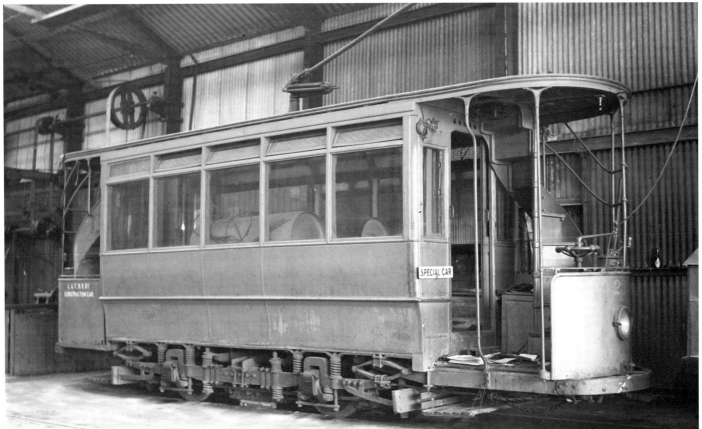

***Above*: Pictured in** Fawcett Street during August 1947 is Sunderland No 100. This tram had originally been MET No 331 and, after 1933, LPTB No 2168. When the production batch of 'Feltham' trams was ordered by the LUT and MET, Charles J. Spencer, tramway manager of the latter, also gained permission for a single centre-entrance to be constructed by UCC at the same time. The development of the 'Feltham' type owed much to Spencer's investigations into overseas practices and the use of centre entrances was one that he was keen to pursue. The result was No 331, which was fitted with UCC-built bogies and which entered service in 1931. However, the decision by the LPTB to convert the London system to trolleybus operation rendered No 331 obsolete as its design precluded its use over the conduit system; the north London routes, largely overhead, were due to be converted first and the more modern trams – such as the 'Felthams' – transferred south of the river where much of the network was conduit. As a result, No 331 was withdrawn in August 1936 and sold to Sunderland the following year. As with a number of other Sunderland trams, No 100 – seen here in August 1947 – was stored during the Second World War and, as the system contracted post-war, the tram was finally withdrawn in 1951. It was acquired for preservation and, after storage, was to reach the museum at Crich in 1961. *Ian L. Wright/Online Transport Archive*

***Opposite above*: During the** late 1930s, the LPTB undertook a policy of converting the bulk of its tramway network north of the river to trolleybus operation; this inevitably resulted in the withdrawal and disposal of a significant number of trams, a number of which were comparatively new. Amongst the casualties was a batch of eight trams that had been new to Ilford Corporation – the last new trams acquired by the corporation – in 1932 and had passed to the LPTB the following year. Ilford Nos 33 (ii) to 40 (ii) were built by Brush on Peckham P22 four-wheel trucks; they retained their original fleet numbers after the LPTB take-over. No 33 is pictured here in Ilford Broadway in August 1933, shortly after the creation of the LPTB, still in its original corporation livery. *Barry Cross Collection/ Online Transport Archive*

***Opposite below*: Withdrawn during** 1937 and 1938, the eight ex-Ilford cars were sold to Sunderland Corporation, fitted with enclosed lower-deck platforms and entered service on Wearside as Nos 2-9. No 3 is seen at the Seaburn terminus in August 1947. All eight were fitted with replacement M&T trucks between 1946 and 1948. Six of the batch were withdrawn as a result of the conversion of the Durham Road route in March 1954, leaving Nos 2 and 5 to survive until the system's final closure. *Ian L. Wright/Online Transport Archive*

Above: Following the final conversion of the Dunfermline & District Tramways Co system on 4 July 1937, the Giant's Causeway, Portrush & Bush Valley Railway & Tramway Co Ltd acquired two of the redundant 3ft 6in gauge trams. One of these, of which little is known, was scrapped before use but the second – Dunfermline No 34 (one of a batch of fifteen cars – Nos 29-43 built by UEC in 1917 on UEC-built four-wheel trucks) – was to become Giant's Causeway No 24. Prior to entering service in June 1938, the tram was re-gauged to 3ft 0in and was converted to single deck. In addition, the end platforms were shortened and each end provided with an enclosed vestibule. As such, the car – seen here at the Giant's Causeway terminus on 7 June 1948 – was to survive through until the final closure of the line on 20 September 1949. *John Meredith/Online Transport Archive*

Opposite above: The last new trams to be acquired by Huddersfield Corporation were eight fully-enclosed cars that were delivered in 1931 – Nos 137-42 – and 1932 – Nos 143 and 144; No 141 – later Sunderland No 30 – is illustrated here. They were constructed by English Electric and fitted with M&T swing-link trucks. However, a change of manager in Huddersfield and the decision to adopt the trolleybus meant that the system was progressively converted between 1933 and final abandonment on 29 June 1940. The eight cars were not, however, to survive in the West Riding until the final closure of the system; they were withdrawn in 1938. *W.A. Camwell/ Online Transport Archive*

Opposite below: Recorded on Fulwell Road in April 1954 is Sunderland Corporation No 34; this was one of eight – Nos 29-36 – fully-enclosed double-deck cars acquired from Huddersfield Corporation in 1938 at £225 each plus £75 for the spares. The eight cars had to be converted from 4ft 7¾in to standard gauge as well as being fitted with pantographs in place of their original trolleypoles. They also lost their mechanical brake fittings, platform doors and route number boxes before re-entering service. No 29 was the first to be withdrawn – in April 1953 – but the remaining cars survived until the final conversion of the Sunderland system on 1 October 1954 with four of the batch – Nos 31, 32, 34 and 35 – featuring in the final closure procession. *Phil Tatt/Online Transport Archive*

Above: **In 1939,** Leeds Corporation acquired three 'HR/2' cars from the LPTB. The three – LT Nos 1881, 1883 and 1886 – were part of a batch of fifty cars supplied by Hurst Nelson in 1930 on EMB LCC Class 6A radial bogies. Becoming Leeds Nos 277-79 respectively, the trio entered service in the West Riding during the early months of the Second World War. No 277 – seen here outside Headingley depot on 25 September 1952 in the then newly introduced predominantly red livery – was the first of the trio to be withdrawn; it succumbed in October 1956 as a result of accident damage that resulted from a collision with 'Horsfield' No 171. The remaining two cars were both withdrawn the following year as the Leeds system contracted. Leeds was interested in the possible purchase of further 'HR/2s'; however, the onset of the Second World War and the delay to the London tramway conversion programme meant that the trams were required for a further decade in the Metropolis. *Julian Thompson/Online Transport Archive*

Opposite above: **The Second** World War placed a serious strain on public transport in Britain; not only was there the very serious threat that enemy action could cause disruption and damage, but demand for services, in an era when fuel rationing restricted severely private motoring and the war economy was placing heavy demands on the population, meant that existing fleets were not always adequate. As one of the country's primary producers of steel, Sheffield was an obvious target for the Luftwaffe and a number of trams were destroyed or seriously damaged. As a result, in 1941, Sheffield Corporation acquired fourteen trams from Newcastle Corporation. These were from a batch of twenty open-top cars – Nos 111-130 – built by Hurst Nelson on Brill 27G four-wheel trucks in 1901. During their Newcastle career, they had been fitted with open balcony top covers but before entering service in Sheffield they were all rebuilt as fully enclosed. The ex-Newcastle trams were destined to survive a decade in Sheffield; the purchase of the post-war 'Roberts' cars – Nos 501-36 – resulted in their demise during 1950 and 1951. Here, No 313 – ex Newcastle No 113 - is seen in Fitzalan Square. *C. Carter/Online Transport Archive*

Opposite below: **Between 1903** and 1915, Hull Corporation acquired seventy-nine open-balcony four-wheel trams (Nos 102-80); these were constructed by G.F. Milnes & Co, UEC, Brush and the corporation itself. Between 1920 and 1931, Nos 102-16/23-36 were modified to become fully enclosed and between 1933 and 1935 Nos 117-22/38-40/42/44-56/58-60/63/64/69/70/73-76 were similarly modified. Two new trams – the last that the corporation acquired – were delivered as fully enclosed in 1923 (No 101 [ii]) and 1925 (113 [ii]). The conversion of the Hull system to trolleybus operation commenced in 1937 and, by the start of the war in 1939, only three routes remained operational . In this view – taken at the Osborne Street terminus of the Dairycoates service, the last to operate in the city – No 176 is closest to the camera; this was one of the last batch of open-balcony cars – Nos 161-80 – supplied by Brush in 1915 on Brill 21E trucks; neither No 176, nor No 148 seen in the background, were amongst the cars to be acquired by Leeds orporation. No 148 was one of twenty-four cars – Nos 137-60 – supplied by Brush in 1912 again on Brill 21E trucks. *W.A. Camwell/National Tramway Museum*

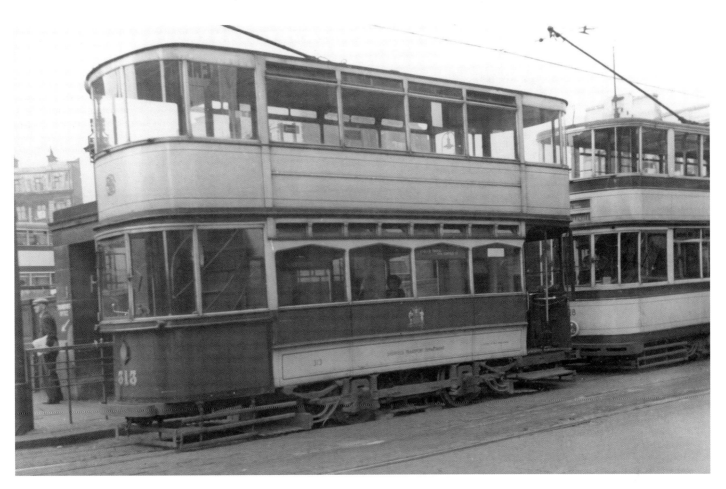

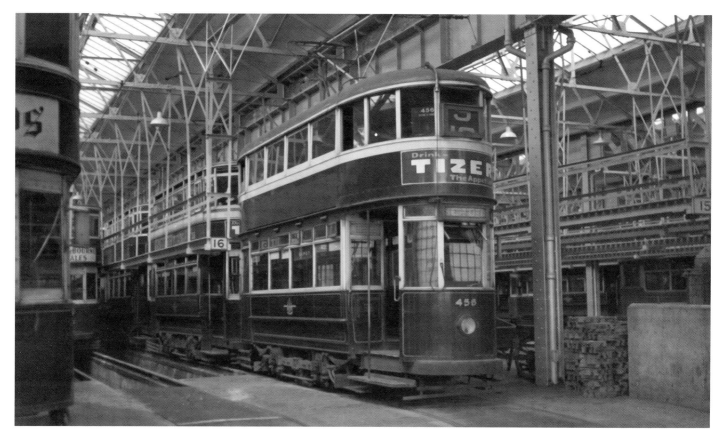

Above: **Leeds Corporation** No 456 – ex-Hull Corporation No 125 – is seen inside Swinegate depot in early June 1950. Early in the war, Leeds was seeking second-hand trams to replace part of its fleet of open-balcony cars; Hull had retained – on the instructions of the Ministry of War Transport – a number of fully-enclosed cars as a reserve following the conversions of the routes along Holderness Road on 17 February 1940 and Anlaby Road on 5 September 1942 and, in 1942, Leeds agreed to purchase thirty-two of these cars and, following the final conversion of the Hull system on 30 June 1945, a further ten followed. The trams had originally been open balcony when new but had been converted to fully enclosed by 1935 and were all fitted with 21E-type four-wheel truck from a variety of manufacturers. No 456 was new originally in 1909 and was one of a batch constructed by G.F. Milnes & Co. The ex-Hull cars were not to survive long in Leeds; the first withdrawal – due to a broken axle – was No 451 in 1945 and all had been withdrawn by the end of 1951; No 456 was withdrawn in April of that year. No 446 – ex-Hull No 132 – was stored for a number of years before being preserved in 1955; it is currently on display in Hull. *Peter N. Williams/Online Transport Archive*

Opposite above: **In order** to supplement its fleet further and to replace trams destroyed by enemy action, Sheffield had already acquired a batch of trams from Newcastle. In 1942 a further ten trams were obtained, this time from Bradford Corporation, which were to become Sheffield Nos 325-34, where they had been rendered surplus due to the conversion of the short section beyond Bradford Moor to Stanningley on 19 October 1942 due to the poor condition of the track. All were built originally by English Electric between 1919 and 1921 and were fitted with Brill 21E four-wheel trucks. Prior to re-entering service, the trucks were re-gauged from 4ft 0in to standard gauge and the open upper-deck balconies were fully enclosed as evinced in this view of No 331 – ex-Bradford No 257 – seen outside Tinsley depot post-war. The ten cars were to survive in Sheffield until withdrawal during 1950 and 1951; one of the batch – No 330 – was converted into a single-deck works cars on withdrawal and, as such, was to survive through to the final conversion of the Sheffield system in October 1960 and was subsequently to be preserved. It now forms part of the NTM collection. *F.N.T. Lloyd-Jones/Online Transport Archive*

Opposite below: **In 1942,** in order to supplement its fleet during the Second World War, Rotherham Corporation hired Leeds Corporation No 125A. This car originally dated to 1908 when, as No 125, it had been constructed at Kirkstall Road Works on a Brill 21E four-wheel truck. Built with an open balcony top deck body and open lower deck vestibules, the car was fitted with enclosed lower-deck vestibules prior to the First World War and was renumbered 125A in 1925. It was in this condition when hired by Rotherham but was converted to fully-enclosed and renumbered 14 prior to entering service. Purchased outright by Rotherham in 1948, the tram was withdrawn with the final conversion of the Rotherham system on 13 November 1949 and subsequently scrapped. It is pictured here outside the corporation's depot at Rawmarsh Road alongside No 12; this was the sole survivor of the corporation's original fleet of tramcars following the delivery of the 11 single-ended cars during 1934 and 1935. *R.J.S. Wiseman*

Above: **For the** opening of its system in 1903, Bury Corporation acquired fourteen open-top bogie cars – Nos 1-14 – and fourteen open-top four-wheel cars – Nos 15-28 – from G.F. Milnes & Co. All of the bogies cars along with four of the four-wheel cars were rebuilt as fully-enclosed during 1925 and 1926. The latter were Nos 15 and 21 plus two others that were to become Nos 30 (ii) and 38 (ii). Of these, one – No 15 – was withdrawn before the Second World War and one – No 30 – was sold to Sunderland in 1948. No 38 remained with Bury Corporation until withdrawal in 1949 but No 21 was sold to Bolton Corporation – where it became No 331 – in 1943. Prior to re-entering service, it had its original four-wheel truck replaced by a Bolton 21E. The tram is pictured here in its final Bury Corporation condition. *W.A. Camwell/National Tramway Museum*

Opposite above: **In 1925,** Bury Corporation acquired a batch of six fully-enclosed trams from English Electric; Nos 55-60 were fitted the same manufacturer's Burnley-style bogies and were the last new trams bought by the corporation. In 1943, three of the batch – Nos 55, 56 and 58 – were acquired by Bolton Corporation, where they became Nos 451-53; the first of the trio is seen here in Bolton still showing its original Bury fleet number. The remaining three cars remained with Bury, where they were to survive until the final conversion of the system on 13 February 1949. As such, they outlived the trio that went to Bolton; the last Bolton trams operated on 29 March 1947. *Barry Cross Collection/Online Transport Archive*

Opposite below: **One section** of the Sunderland system – the Villette Road route – required the use of single-deck trams as a result of a low railway bridge. For a brief period, from 27 August 1930, the service was suspended as no suitable trams for its operation were available. This was rectified by the delivery of No 85 from Brush in 1931, with the Villette Road route being reinstated in March that year. Fitted with the same manufacturer's maximum traction bogies, the car was one of a number that were stored following the outbreak of war in September 1939; it was destined never to operate again in Sunderland. *Barry Cross Collection/Online Transport Archive*

Opposite: **In October** 1944, Leeds Corporation acquired Sunderland Corporation single-deck car No 85 for £375. Initially allocated the fleet number 288 in the West Riding, the car was little used. The car's original bogies were unsatisfactory and so were replaced during the summer of 1945 by the ex-LCC 6A radial bogies from 'HR/2' No 279. Further testing resulted in problems being identified and the tram was stored from mid-1946 on a spare set of EMB heavyweight bogies in Kirkstall Works painted in a dark grey undercoat with cream window surrounds and it is in this condition that the car is recorded here. In December 1947, it was stored at Torre Road before returning to Kirkstall Works in the summer of 1948 and used in further tests, this time actually bearing the fleet number 288, during the autumn of the same year. *F.E.J. Ward/Online Transport Archive*

Above: **Following the** tests in late 1948, work started on the conversion of No 288 into the first of three experimental single-deck cars – No 600 – for use in the tramway subways that Leeds Corporation was proposing at the time. Work was protracted, however, and the rebuilt car was not to emerge until February 1953 (for tests; it did not actually enter service until the summer of 1954). It is in its rebuilt guise that the car was photographed at the terminus of the Hunslet route in April 1955. Unfortunately, however, a change of political power resulted in the abandonment of the subway plans and the conversion of the Leeds system. As a result the three single-deck cars eked out their existence and No 600 was last used in service in September 1957. Still extant at the system's closure on 7 November 1959, the tram was acquired for preservation the following year and now forms part of the NTM collection. *Phil Tatt/Online Transport Archive*

Above: **Alongside the** passenger cars acquired from Hull Corporation in 1942 and 1945, Leeds Corporation also bought the latter's single-deck works car, No 96, which entered service in Leeds in July 1945. The car was new originally in 1901 and was one of a batch – Nos 91-100 – supplied by Hurst Nelson on Brill 21E four-wheel trucks; converted to single-deck in 1933, No 96 was then employed as a snowplough through until the final conversion of the Hull system on 30 June 1945. Renumbered 6 by Leeds, the car was used primarily as a snow plough until February 1949 and then as a stores car until rail grinding equipment was installed in 1954. It is pictured here in the Sovereign Street Permanent Way Yard in April 1954; surviving until the closure of the system, No 6 was the last tram to run through the streets of Leeds when it was towed from the PW Yard to Swinegate on 8 December. Preserved, the car is now based on the Heaton Park Tramway in Manchester. *Phil Tatt/Online Transport Archive*

Opposite above: **Following the** final closure of the Oldham Corporation system on 3 August 1946, six of the redundant trams were acquired by the Gateshead & District Tramways Co. These fully-enclosed double-deck cars fitted with Preston 21E four-wheel trucks had been new originally in 1924 (Nos 17, 18 and 24) and 1926 (Nos 122, 125 and 128). These were to become Gateshead Nos 35, 72, 71, 68-70 respectively with the first, No 68, entering service on Tyneside in early 1947. All six survived until March 1951 when, following the conversion of the Saltwell Park route (on which the ex-Oldham cars operated latterly), all of the surviving double-deck cars were withdrawn and scrapped. Pictured at the terminus of the Saltwell Park route towards the end of its operation is No 69; this had originally been Oldham No 125. *R.W.A. Jones/Online Transport Archive*

Opposite below: **Although a** relatively small system, Darwen Corporation operated a joint service with neighbouring Blackburn Corporation and, in 1936, acquired two modern streamlined trams – Nos 23 and 24 – from English Electric that were fitted with the same manufacturer's maximum traction bogies. Although the corporation had tried to abandon its surviving tramways during the Second World War, this had been rejected by the Ministry of War Transport and, as a result, it was not until 5 October 1946 that the surviving section from the town centre to the borough boundary was converted to bus operation. The two streamlined cars were, however, not to survive until the end, having been sold earlier in the year to the L&CBER, where they were to be renumbered 24 and 23 respectively and re-gauged from 4ft 0in to 3ft 6in. Unfortunately for the L&CBER, restrictions on the use of fully-enclosed trams on exposed and hilly sections of 3ft 6in gauge systems meant that the cars were limited in their operation in North Wales. Both were withdrawn in 1953 but not finally scrapped until after the system closed on 24 March 1956. During the summer of 1951, No 24 – ex-Darwen No 23 – is recorded standing outside the company's Rhos-on-Sea depot. *Phil Tatt/Online Transport Archive*

Above: **Although the** bulk of the South Shields Corporation network was converted to trolleybus operation before the Second World War one route – that from Moon Street to Cleadon – was retained and was to survive until 1 April 1946. A number of second-hand trams were acquired in the early 1930s and, in 1936, English Electric supplied the corporation's last new tram – the streamlined No 52 – that was fitted with an M&T swing-link four-wheel truck. No 52 was acquired by Sunderland Corporation following the final conversion in South Shields and became No 48 on Wearside. It is seen here at the Grangetown terminus and was to survive until withdrawal following the conversion of the Durham Road route in March 1954. *R.W.A. Jones/Online Transport Archive*

Opposite above: **The 'Pilcher'** or 'Pullman' trams were the last new cars to be built for Manchester Corporation; named after the general manager – Stuart Pilcher – thirty-eight trams were constructed by Manchester on Peckham P35 trucks between March 1930 and October 1932. The cars were acquired as a result of a recommendation made by Pilcher to the corporation's Tramways Committee on 21 February 1929 that a batch of four-wheel cars be constructed for operation primarily on those joint services where the other operators used four-wheel trams. In 1946, with the corporation reconfirming its policy of tramcar conversion, the thirty-eight cars were offered for sale. Here No 270, which was to become Aberdeen Corporation No 48 (ii) in 1948, is seen on an enthusiasts' tour. *F.N.T. Lloyd-Jones/Online Transport Archive*

Opposite below: **The first** purchaser of the 'Pilcher' cars from Manchester was Leeds Corporation, which eventually acquired seven of the batch at £200 each. In early 1946, the corporation decided on the possible purchase of fifty new double-deck trams. However, for a variety of reasons, the trams were not ordered and, as a result, alternatives were sought. Manchester No 287 was brought across the Pennines in 1946 and, after a successful trial, a further six were acquired. These all entered service during 1948 and 1949 but were not to survive for long. No 284 was withdrawn in 1951 and the remainder had all been taken out of service by April 1954. No 283 – recorded at the Hunslet terminus of route 25 on 9 June 1951 – was originally Manchester No 266 – the prototype of the 'Pilcher' class – and was withdrawn in August 1953. *Julian Thompson/Online Transport Archive*

Above: **Sunderland Corporation** acquired six of the ex-Manchester 'Pilcher' cars for £200 apiece; these became Nos 37-42 on Wearside and entered service – having been fitted with pantographs in place of their original trolleypoles – during 1947. Here, No 42 – ex-Manchester No 131 – is pictured in April 1953 at the Roker terminus prior to heading south with a service on the Circle route. Two of the sextet were withdrawn during the first half of 1953; the remaining four cars – including No 42 – survived into January 1954. *Phil Tatt/Online Transport Archive*

Opposite above: **Recorded at** Levenhall on 5 August 1947 when virtually newly in service is Edinburgh No 401; this was the first of eleven ex-Manchester 'Pilcher' cars that entered service in the Scottish capital between 1947 and 1949. Nine of the cars cost £210 each but two – Nos 173 and 676 – had been slightly damaged before withdrawal in Manchester and so were sold for £173 and £175 respectively. When they were purchased, the Edinburgh system seemed to have a secure future, but this was not to last and all of the 'Pilchers' were withdrawn by the end of 1954, two years before the final abandonment of the Edinburgh system. No 401 had originally been Manchester No 173 and was new in 1931. *Michael H. Waller*

Opposite below: **The last** second-hand tram acquired by Sunderland Corporation was No 85 – seen here at the terminus of the Southwick route during the period when the route was operated as a shuttle between March and September 1951 when the railway bridge on the route was declared unsafe – which was acquired from Bury Corporation in 1948. During the 1920s, Bury rebuilt four trams that dated originally to a batch of four-wheel open-top trams – Nos 15-28 – that were supplied by G.F. Milnes & Co in 1903. Two of the modified trams – Nos 30 (ii) and 38 (ii) – were renumbered when rebuilt and their original fleet numbers are uncertain. It was No 30 that Sunderland acquired. Fitted with an EMB four-wheel truck, No 85 was to survive until the conversion of the Durham Road route in March 1954. *R.W.A. Jones/Online Transport Archive*

Above: **In 1948,** the newly-nationalised Grimsby & Immingham Electric Railway acquired three single-deck cars from Newcastle Corporation (Nos 29, 42 and 77). The three cars, which became Grimsby & Immingham Nos 6-8, were from a batch of sixty cars – Nos 29-88 – supplied to the corporation by Hurst Nelson & Co in 1902; initially, all were fitted with Brill 27G bogies but twenty-five – including the three that passed to the Grimsby & Immingham – received replacement Peckham P25 maximum traction bogies and, of these, eight – again including Nos 29, 42 and 77 – were rebodied by the corporation during 1932 and 1933. The ex-Newcastle trams were destined to have a relatively short life on Humberside, being withdrawn in 1953 following the acquisition of additional second-hand trams, this time from Gateshead. Here No 6 – ex-Newcastle No 29 – is seen at the Corporation Bridge terminus in Grimsby on 23 July 1950. *Peter N. Williams/Online Transport Archive*

Opposite: **Apart from** Grimsby & Immingham, the Gateshead & District Tramways Co also acquired a number of trams from Newcastle Corporation in 1948; these comprised the remainder of the eight single-deck cars rebuilt by the corporation during 1932 and 1933 – Nos 43, 52, 54, 80 and 88 – which became Gateshead No 73-77. As a result of the number of cross-river services operated by the corporation and the company, the ex-Newcastle cars continued to venture over the Tyne even after the end of the Newcastle Corporation operation (on 4 March 1951) and here Gateshead No 76 – ex-Newcastle No 54 – is pictured in Newcastle centre towards the end of the company operation. The Dunston service was the last of the Gateshead routes to survive, being converted to bus operation on 4 August 1951. *J. Joyce/Online Transport Archive*

Above: In the late 1940s, Leeds Corporation was seeking additional trams to supplement its fleet and to replace the ex-Hull cars as well as other older cars. Following an advertisement, it was agreed to purchase a number of trams from Southampton Corporation during 1949 and 1950. The Southampton system was being converted to bus operation at the time – the last trams operated in the city on 31 December 1949 – and so its redundant trams were offered for sale. Leeds acquired thirty-seven in total; however, only eleven actually entered service in Leeds and these were the newest of the cars acquired. Of the remainder, eleven were allocated Leeds fleet numbers but were scrapped in 1951 without ever entering service, a further six were transferred to Leeds but were disposed of to a farm in Farsley in 1950 where they were eventually scrapped and the remaining eight were scrapped in Southampton. One factor in this was the decision to acquire the ex-LT 'Feltham' cars. As a result of this and the decision to convert the Leeds system to bus operation, the ex-Southampton cars were destined to have a short working life in the West Riding; all were withdrawn by the end of 1953. No 292 – seen here in City Square in early June 1950 – was originally Southampton No 107 and was new in 1930; like all of the ex-Southampton cars, it was fitted with a Peckham P35 four-wheel truck. The bodywork on the majority of the cars was constructed by Southampton Corporation. *Peter N. Williams/Online Transport Archive*

Opposite: The evolution of the Southampton fully-enclosed four-wheel tram, designed to cope with the low gate of the Bargate (which was only finally bypassed in June 1938), is complex, with numerous cars built or rebuilt and renumbered over the years. Suffice to note here that between 1923 and 1931, more than forty domed-roof cars were constructed in the corporation's workshops and a number of others were so rebuilt. These were fitted with either Brill 21E or Peckham P35 trucks. Two of the type – Nos 108 and 17 (ii) – are pictured at the Royal Pier terminus on 1 June 1947. At this stage, the post-war conversion of the Southampton system had not commenced but, eventually, both trams were acquired by Leeds Corporation. No 108 (one of those constructed during 1929/30 on Pechkham trucks) was one of those that re-entered service in the West Riding, becoming No 290, whilst No 17 (ii) (one of 11 constructed between 1923 and 1929) was, however, one of those that never made the journey northwards and was scrapped in Southampton. *John Meredith/Online Transport Archive*

Above: **The fourth** operator to acquire second-hand 'Pilcher' cars from Manchester Corporation was Aberdeen Corporation that bought fourteen in 1948 at a cost of £300 each; these were destined to become Aberdeen Nos 39-52 and the first of these is seen at the Bridge of Don terminus on 24 January 1949. This tram had originally been Manchester No 121 and new in 1930. The Aberdeen 'Pilchers' were the last of the type to remain in service – being withdrawn during 1955 and 1956 – and there were efforts to try and preserve one. No 49 – ex-Manchester No 106 – was offered for sale for preservation at £50 plus £200 transport costs following withdrawal in June 1956; unfortunately, this was not successful and all of the 'Pilchers' were scrapped. *Michael H. Waller*

Opposite: **During the** 1920s, under the influence of the MET's manager C.J. Spencer, the company experimented with a number of innovative designs of tramcar. This work ultimately culminated in the development and production of the 'Feltham' type of bogie car, of which 100 were built by another subsidiary of the Underground group – the United Construction Co – during 1931. Of these, fifty-four were destined for operation by the MET with the remaining being acquired by LUT. All 100 were to pass to the LPTB in July 1933, with the ex-MET cars (Nos 319/21-29/32-75) becoming LPTB Nos 2066-119 and the ex-LUT cars (Nos 351-96) becoming LPTB Nos 2120-65. As a consequence of the programme of tram to trolleybus conversion north of the river undertaken in the late 1930s, all of the 'Felthams' were transferred to the surviving network south of the river, where they were largely based on services operated out of Telford Avenue (such as routes 16 and 18). Two of the type – Nos 2109 and 2113 – were lost as a result of enemy action; a further six were scrapped by the end of 1949. The final 'Feltham' services – the 16, 18 and 42 – were all converted to bus operation as part of Stage 3 of 'Operation Tramaway' on 7/8 April 1951; by that point, Leeds Corporation had acquired the surviving cars. Here ex-LUT No 2126 – destined to become Leeds No 565 – is seen at the Downton Avenue loading island on Streatham Hill with a service on route 16 on 15 June 1949. *John Meredith/Online Transport Archive*

***Above*: Having acquired** three ex-London Transport 'HR/2' trams in the late 1930s and having appointed Victor Matterface, from London Transport, as its Chief Rolling Stock Engineer, it was perhaps inevitable that Leeds took advantage of the decision to the LTE to reinstate its pre-war programme of tramway conversion to acquire further second-hand trams. Towards the end of 1949, one of the 'Feltham' type – No 2099 – was transferred to the West Riding to test its suitability and for a period it operated in Leeds livery whilst still retaining its original London fleet number; it is seen in this condition at Belle Isle in June 1950. It was eventually agreed that Leeds would acquire the ninety surviving 'Feltham' cars – including No 2099 – as they were withdrawn by London Transport. Unfortunately, two of the cars – Nos 2144 and 2162 – were destroyed by fire before they could be sent northwards. The purchase of the 90 cars represented the single largest second-hand acquisition in the UK. Although all of the ex-MET received in Leeds entered service, a number of the ex-LUT cars were scrapped without operating in the West Riding. Two of the ex-MET cars – Nos 501 and 526 – were preserved and are now based at the London Transport Museum and in the USA respectively; one of the ex-LUT cars was also secured for preservation but, following vandalism on the Middleton Railway, its body was scrapped. Its trucks, however, were retained and are now in use under the restored 'E/1' car No 1622 at Crich. *Peter N. Williams/Online Transport Archive*

***Opposite above*: Although the** majority of the 'Felthams' that travelled to the West Riding finally entered service, a handful were scrapped without ever losing their original London Transport identity. That was the fate of No 2135 – scheduled to be Leeds No 584 – which is seen here being dismantled at Low Fields Road yard in November 1956. *Barry Cross Collection/Online Transport Archive*

Left: Between **1920** and 1928 the Gateshead & District Tramways Co acquired twenty-five new single-deck trams – Nos 1 (ii) to 20 (ii) and 56-60. Of these Nos 1, 20 and 56-60 were constructed by Brush with the remaining cars constructed by the company itself. All were fitted with Brill 39E maximum traction bogies with the exception of Nos 12, 13, 15 and 19, which were equipped with Brill 22E maximum traction bogies. Nos 13 and 15 were initially constructed as open-platform front-exit cars but were equipped with fully-enclosed vestibules during 1926 and 1927. No 9, later to become Grimsby & Immingham No 19 is pictured towards the end of the Gateshead system; the final trams operated in Tyneside on 4 August 1951. *J. Joyce/Online Transport Archive*

Above: **Following the** final conversion of the Gateshead & District system on 4 August 1951, British Railways acquired nineteen of the company's single-deck cars constructed during the 1920s. Of these, seventeen entered service on the Grimsby & Immingham line as Nos 17-33 but an eighteenth – ex-Gateshead No 4 – was seriously damaged in transit and was scrapped without re-entering service. Their arrival supplemented the existing fleet whilst permitting the withdrawal of the ex-Newcastle cars, Nos 6-8 (in 1954), and four of the original ex-Great Central fleet. As one of the mainstays of the service, the ex-Gateshead cars survived until the closure of the Grimsby & Immingham 1 July 1961. Here, No 22 – ex-Gateshead No 7 of 1928 – is seen at the Immingham Docks terminus. Two of the type – Grimsby & Immingham Nos 20 (ex-Gateshead No 5) and 26 (ex-Gateshead 10) were preserved on withdrawal and are now part of the collections at Crich and Beamish respectively. *J. Joyce/Online Transport Archive*

Opposite: **The eighteenth** ex-Gateshead car to enter service on the Grimsby & Immingham line in 1951 was converted into a works car – No DE320224 – and replaced ex-Great Central No 5, which had been retained on the line since the rest of the batch had been withdrawn in 1931 specifically for work duties. Here, the replacement works car is seen outside the line's workshops at Pyewipe alongside the line's tower wagon showing to good effect the sliding doors added to facilitate its new duties; as Gateshead No 17, the tram was new originally in 1927 and was to survive on Humberside until the Immingham line's final closure. It was subsequently scrapped. *Ronnie Stephens/Online Transport Archive*

Above: **No 1** was the most advanced tramcar built for the LCC and entered service originally in June 1932. Constructed by the LCC itself on EMB Type 6A radial bogies, the car was designed as a prototype for replacing the LCC's ageing fleet. Unfortunately, the creation of the LPTB in 1933 and its decision to convert the tram network to trolleybus operation rendered No 1 irrelevant but it continued to operate in the Metropolis until withdrawal in April 1951. The tram is seen here at the Wimbledon terminus of routes 2 and 4 on an LRTL tour with two service cars in the background and, beyond, two trolleybuses. *F.NT. Lloyd-Jones/Online Transport Archive*

Opposite: **Following the** loss of two of the 'Felthams' – Nos 2144 and 2162 – that Leeds had bought, Victor Matterface sought a replacement in the guise of ex-LCC No 1 *Bluebird* (although this was not in compensation for the two lost cars but part of a separate transaction and cost Leeds £500 to purchase; I am grateful to Dave Jones of the LCCTT for the information on this sale). Entering service in the West Riding in December 1951 as Leeds No 301, the tram – which is seen here outside Kirkstall Road Works in April 1954 – was latterly to spend most of its life operating peak hour only services until withdrawal, following the conversion of the Dewsbury Road and Moortown route, in September 1957. Preserved initially as part of the BTC collection, the car was eventually to become part of the NTM collection and is, at the time of writing, undergoing a complete restoration. *Phil Tatt/Online Transport Archive*

Above: **During 1936** and 1937, a total of 163 streamlined bogie cars were constructed for Liverpool Corporation to the design of R.J. Heathman at Edge Lane Works. The type was to suffer a number of losses during the 1940s, primarily as a result of two depot fires at Green Lane in 1942 (which resulted in the destruction of Nos 171 and 989) and in 1947, when Nos 159/63/73, 876/82/88/92/94-96/98, 908/12/15/59/60/80/87/91 were destroyed. The bogies from a number of the cars lost in 1947 were sold to Glasgow and Leeds corporations. With the rapid conversion of the Liverpool system to bus operation during the late 1940s and early 1950s, a number of the surviving cars were to become surplus to requirements and were acquired by Glasgow Corporation. Liverpool No 899 – seen inbound on route 29 at Lower House Lane on 3 April 1954 – was sold to Glasgow Corporation in 1954 and became No 1031 (ii) north of the border. It was to survive in service until 1960. *John McCann/Online Transport Archive*

Opposite above: **Glasgow Corporation** acquired six sets of EMB bogies from Liverpool Corporation in 1948; one set was used on 'Coronation' No 1179 between 1951 and 1954 but between July and October 1954 all six sets were utilised in the completion of six replacement 'Coronation' cars – Nos 1393-98 – that were built to replace a number of earlier cars of the type that had been destroyed as a result of the Newlands Depot fire of 11 April 1948. The first of the batch is seen here at Mosspark in August 1954 when almost brand-new. Towards the end of No 1398's career – in March 1961 – it received replacement Glasgow motors and bogies. It was withdrawn the following month. Four of the batch were taken out of service during 1961, leaving Nos 1394 and 1398 to soldier on until October 1962 and November 1962 respectively. *Phil Tatt/Online Transport Archive*

Opposite below: **In the** early 1950s one of the most secure – and certainly the largest – system was that of Glasgow Corporation. Although there had been some contraction – most notably as a result of the introduction of trolleybuses in 1949 – there was still no overall plan to convert the remaining system. There was, however, a realisation that the fleet, despite the construction of the post-war 'Cunarder' cars, was getting elderly and needed replacement. With the rapid contraction of the Liverpool Corporation system, there were available a significant number of modern streamlined bogie cars and, mid-1953, Glasgow purchased twenty-four at £500 apiece (including delivery). These initial cars had all been built by Liverpool at Edge Lane Works on M&T swinglink bogies; as Glasgow Nos 1006-16/18-30, these trams entered service on Clydeside between December 1953 and April 1954. At about the same time, it became clear that additional trams were going to become available and, in late 1954, a further twenty-two were purchased at £580 each; these became Nos 1031-38/41-59/52-56. The major difference between the two batches was that the later cars – which entered service between September 1954 and May 1956 – were fitted with a mix of EMB Lightweight and Heavyweight bogies. Unfortunately, in late 1954 and early 1955 the process that led, eventually to the conversion of the Glasgow system commenced and so the ex-Liverpool cars were destined for a short life in Glasgow; they were all withdrawn between 1958 and July 1960 with one – Glasgow No 1055 (ex-Liverpool No 869) being preserved. In this view No 1020 (ex-Liverpool No 937) is seen at the Tollcross terminus of route 29 on 22 May 1954. The car was relatively new at that date, having entered service in Glasgow during January 1954; it was to be one of the earliest casualties, being withdrawn in October 1958. *Michael H. Waller*

APPENDIX

Original fleet	Original fleet number	Entered Service	Withdrawn	Second/third fleet	Second/third fleet number	Into service	Withdrawn	Notes
Accrington	28	1915	1932	Llandudno & Colwyn Bay	1 (ii)	1933	1956	
Accrington	29	1915	1932	Llandudno & Colwyn Bay	2 (ii)	1933	1956	
Accrington	30	1915	1932	Llandudno & Colwyn Bay	3 (ii)	1933	1956	
Accrington	31	1920	1932	Llandudno & Colwyn Bay	4 (ii)	1933	1956	
Accrington	32	1920	1932	Llandudno & Colwyn Bay	5 (ii)	1933	1956	
Accrington	38	1915	1932	Southend-on-Sea	66	1934	1942	
Accrington	39	1915	1932	Lytham St Annes	55	1933	1937	
Accrington	40	1920	1932	Southend-on-Sea	67	1934	1942	
Accrington	41	1920	1932	Southend-on-Sea	68	1934	1942	
Accrington	42	1926	1931	Sunderland	19 (ii)	1931	1953	
Accrington	43	1926	1931	Sunderland	20 (ii)	1931	1953	
Alexandra Palace	Unknown	1898	1901	Great Grimsby	25	1901	By 1929	
Alexandra Palace	Unknown	1898	1901	Great Grimsby	26	1901	By 1929	
Alexandra Palace	Unknown	1898	1901	Great Grimsby	27	1901	1930	
Alexandra Palace	Unknown	1898	1901	Great Grimsby	28	1901	By 1929	
Ayr	29	1928	1932	South Shields	54	1932	1946	Ex-Dumbarton; renumbered 16 (ii) in 1934. Rebuilt as fully enclosed
Ayr	30	1928	1932	South Shields	57	1932	1937/38	Ex-Dumbarton; renumbered 34 (ii) in 1934

Barking	8	1911	1915	Ilford	28	1915	1930	Initially hired and then purchased
Barking	9	1911	1915	East Ham	46	1915	1935	Became LPTB No 70 in 1933
Barking	10	1912	1914	Ilford	27	1914	1938	Became LPTB No 31 in 1933
Birmingham	21-300 batch	1905	1933	Dover	19 (ii)	1933	1936	
Birmingham	21-300 batch	1905-08	1933	Dover	20 (ii)	1933	1936	
Birmingham	21-300 batch	1905-08	1933	Dover	21 (ii)	1933	1936	
Birmingham	21-300 batch	1905-08	1933	Dover	22 (ii)	1933	1936	
Birmingham	21-300 batch	1905-08	1933	Merthyr	3 (ii)	1933	1939	
Birmingham	21-300 batch	1905-08	1933	Merthyr	4 (ii)	1933	1939	
Birmingham	21-300 batch	1905-08	1933	Merthyr	6 (ii)	1933	1939	
Birmingham	226	1907	1933	Merthyr	12 (ii)	1933	1939	
Birmingham & Midland	15	1915	1928	Dover	11 (ii)	1928	1936	
Birmingham & Midland	17	1915	1928	Dover	12 (ii)	1928	1936	
Birmingham & Midland	Unknown	1913-16	1929/30	Merthyr	2 (ii)	1929/30	1939	Body fitted onto ex-Merthyr truck
Birmingham & Midland	Unknown	1913-16	1929/30	Merthyr	7 (ii)	1929/30	1939	Body fitted onto ex-Merthyr truck
Birmingham & Midland	Unknown	1913-16	1929/30	Merthyr	8 (ii)	1929/30	1939	Body fitted onto ex-Merthyr truck
Birmingham & Midland	Unknown	1913-16	1929/30	Merthyr	9 (ii)	1929/30	1939	Body fitted onto ex-Merthyr truck
Birmingham & Midland	Unknown	1913-16	1929/30	Merthyr	11 (ii)	1929/30	1939	Body fitted onto ex-Merthyr truck
Birmingham & Midland	Unknown	1913-16	1929/30	Merthyr	13 (ii)	1929/30	1939	Body fitted onto ex-Merthyr truck
Birmingham & Midland	Unknown	1913-16	1929/30	Merthyr	14 (ii)	1929/30	1939	Body fitted onto ex-Merthyr truck
Birmingham & Midland	Unknown	1913-16	1929/30	Merthyr	15 (ii)	1929/30	1939	Body fitted onto ex-Merthyr truck
Birmingham & Midland	Unknown	1913-16	1929/30	Merthyr	16 (ii)	1929/30	1939	Body fitted onto ex-Merthyr truck
Birmingham & Midland	Unknown	1904 (rebuilt 1915)	1930	Dover	6 (ii)	1930	1936	

Original fleet	Original fleet number	Entered Service	Withdrawn	Second/third fleet	Second / third fleet number	Into service	Withdrawn	Notes
Birmingham & Midland	Unknown	1904 (rebuilt 1915)	1930	Dover	7 (ii)	1930	1936	
Birmingham & Midland	Unknown	1904 (rebuilt 1915)	1930	Dover	10 (ii)	1930	1936	
Birmingham & Midland	Unknown	1913	1930	Dover	14 (ii)	1930	1936	
Birmingham & Midland	Unknown	1904 (rebuilt 1915)	1930	Dover	17 (ii)	1930	1936	
Bournemouth	55	1901		Llandudno & Colwyn Bay	23 (ii)	1936	1956	Originally delivered to the Poole & District Tramways Co Ltd; was eventually renumbered 23A
Bournemouth	85	1914		Llandudno & Colwyn Bay	6 (ii)	1936	1955	Preserved; now based at NTM
Bournemouth	95	1921		Llandudno & Colwyn Bay	11 (ii)	1936	1956	
Bournemouth	103	1921		Llandudno & Colwyn Bay	10 (ii)	1936	1956	
Bournemouth	108	1921		Llandudno & Colwyn Bay	9 (ii)	1936	1956	
Bournemouth	112	1921		Llandudno & Colwyn Bay	13 (ii)	1936	1956	
Bournemouth	114	1924-26		Llandudno & Colwyn Bay	15 (ii)	1936	1956	
Bournemouth	115	1924-26		Llandudno & Colwyn Bay	14 (ii)	1936	1956	
Bournemouth	116	1924-26		Llandudno & Colwyn Bay	7 (ii)	1936	1956	
Bournemouth	121	1924-26		Llandudno & Colwyn Bay	8 (ii)	1936	1956	
Bournemouth	128	1924-26		Llandudno & Colwyn Bay	12 (ii)	1936	1956	
Bradford	214	1921	1942	Sheffield	325	1943	1951	
Bradford	215	1921	1942	Sheffield	332	1943	1950	
Bradford	216	1921	1942	Sheffield	328	1943	1950	
Bradford	217	1921	1942	Sheffield	334	1943	1951	
Bradford	219	1921	1942	Sheffield	333	1943	1951	
Bradford	237	1919	1942	Sheffield	329	1943	1950	
Bradford	242	1919	1942	Sheffield	327	1943	1950	
Bradford	243	1919	1942	Sheffield	326	1943	1949	

Bradford	251	1920	1942	Sheffield	330	1943	1951	Converted to works car. Preserved on withdrawal; now based at NTM
Bradford	257	1920	1942	Sheffield	331	1943	1951	
Burton & Ashby	1-20 batch	1905/06	1927	Tynemouth & District	22	1927	1931	Renumbered 1 (ii) c1927
Burton & Ashby	1-20 batch	1905/06	1927	Tynemouth & District	23	1927	1931	Renumbered 6 (ii) c1927
Burton & Ashby	1-20 batch	1905/06	1927	Tynemouth & District	24	1927	1931	Acquired but not operated
Burton & Ashby	1-20 batch	1905/06	1927	Tynemouth & District	N/A	1927	1927	Acquired but not operated
Burton & Ashby	1-20 batch	1905/06	1927	Tynemouth & District	N/A	1927	1927	Acquired but not operated
Burton & Ashby	1-20 batch	1905/06	1927	Tynemouth & District	N/A	1927	1927	Acquired but not operated
Burton & Ashby	1-20 batch	1905/06	1927	Tynemouth & District	N/A	1927	1927	Acquired but not operated
Burton & Ashby	1-20 batch	1905/06	1927	Tynemouth & District	N/A	1927	1927	Acquired but not operated
Burton & Ashby	1-20 batch	1905/06	1927	Tynemouth & District	N/A	1927	1927	Acquired but not operated
Burton & Ashby	1-20 batch	1905/06	1927	Tynemouth & District	N/A	1927	1927	Acquired but not operated
Burton-on-Trent	21	1920	1930	York	42	1930	1935	
Burton-on-Trent	22	1920	1930	York	43	1930	1935	
Burton-on-Trent	23	1920	1930	York	44	1930	1935	
Burton-on-Trent	24	1920	1930	York	45	1930	1935	
Bury	21	1903	1943	Bolton	331	1943	1947	
Bury	55	1925	1943	Bolton	451	1943	1947	
Bury	56	1925	1943	Bolton	452	1943	1947	
Bury	58	1925	1943	Bolton	453	1943	1947	
Bury	30 (ii)	1903	1948	Sunderland	85 (ii)	1948	1954	
Cavehill & Whitewell	6-10 batch	1906	1912	Mansfield	19	1912	1932	
Cavehill & Whitewell	6-10 batch	1906	1912	Mansfield	20	1912	1932	
Cheltenham & District	24	1921	1921	Leamington & Warwick	14	1921	1930	Ordered by Cheltenham & District but diverted as new to Leamington & Warwick

Original fleet	Original fleet number	Entered Service	Withdrawn	Second/third fleet	Second / third fleet number	Into service	Withdrawn	Notes
Coventry	19	1898	1904	Norwich	41	1904	1935	
City of Birmingham	217-38/43-56 batch	1904	1912	Devonport	26	1912	By 1934	Became Plymouth 66 following take-over in 1915
City of Birmingham	217-38/43-56 batch	1904	1912	Devonport	27	1912	By 1934	Became Plymouth 67 following take-over in 1915
City of Birmingham	217-38/43-56 batch	1904	1912	Devonport	28	1912	By 1934	Became Plymouth 68 following take-over in 1915
City of Birmingham	217-38/43-56 batch	1904	1912	Devonport	29	1912	By 1934	Became Plymouth 69 in 1915
City of Birmingham	189-92 batch	1902	1912	Devonport	30	1912	By 1925	Ex-Sheerness car' Became Plymouth 70 following take-over in 1915
City of Birmingham	151-71 batch	1901/02	1912	Devonport	31	1912	By 1935	Became Plymouth 71 following take-over in 1915; renumbered 41 in 1922
City of Birmingham	151-71 batch	1901/02	1912	Devonport	32	1912	By 1935	Became Plymouth 72 following take-over in 1915
City of Birmingham	151-71 batch	1901/02	1912	Devonport	33	1912	By 1935	Became Plymouth 73 following take-over in 1915; renumbered 42 in 1922
Coventry	20	1898	1904	Norwich	42	1904	1935	
Croydon	56	1902	1906	South Met	27	1906	Circa 1930	
Croydon	57	1902	1906	South Met	28	1906	1931	
Croydon	58	1902	1906	South Met	29	1906	1931	
Croydon	59	1902	1906	South Met	31	1906	1931	
Croydon	60	1902	1906	South Met	35	1906	1931	
Darlington	17	1913	1926	Dover	8 (ii)	1926	1936	
Darlington	18	1913	1926	Dover	9 (ii)	1926	1936	

Darwen	23	1936	1946	Llandudno & Colwyn Bay	24	1946	1953	Converted from 4ft 0in to 3ft 6in
Darwen	24	1936	1946	Llandudno & Colwyn Bay	23 (iii)	1946	1953	Converted from 4ft 0in to 3ft 6in
Dearne District	1-30 batch	1923/24	1933	Lytham St Annes	51	1933	1937	
Dearne District	1-30 batch	1923/24	1933	Lytham St Annes	52	1933	1937	
Dearne District	1-30 batch	1923/24	1933	Lytham St Annes	53	1933	1937	
Dearne District	1-30 batch	1923/24	1933	Lytham St Annes	54	1933	1937	
Dearne District	1-30 batch	1923/24	1933	Falkirk &District	11 (ii)	1933	1936	
Dearne District	1-30 batch	1923/24	1933	Falkirk &District	12 (ii)	1933	1936	
Dearne District	1-30 batch	1923/24	1933	Falkirk &District	17 (ii)	1933	1936	
Dearne District	1-30 batch	1923/24	1933	Falkirk &District	18 (ii)	1933	1936	
Dearne District	1-30 batch	1923/24	1933	Falkirk &District	19 (ii)	1933	1936	
Dumbarton	31	1921	1928	Ayr	29	1928	1932	Sold to South Shields
Dumbarton	32	1921	1928	Ayr	30	1928	1932	Sold to South Shields
Dundee	13	1900	1926	Dundee, Broughty Ferry & District	15	1926	1931	
Dundee	16	1900	1926	Dundee, Broughty Ferry & District	16	1926	1931	
Dunfermline & District	34	1917	1937	Giant's Causeway	24	1937	1949	
Dunfermline & District	Unknown	Unknown	1937	Giant's Causeway	N/A	1937	1937	Scrapped without entering service
Erith	15	1906	1915	Dartford	13	1915	1917	Destroyed in depot fire
Erith	16	1906	1915	Doncaster	37	1915	1938	
Exeter	1 (ii)	1929	1931	Halifax	128	1931	1938	
Exeter	2 (ii)	1929	1931	Halifax	129	1931	1938	
Exeter	3 (ii)	1929	1931	Halifax	130	1931	1938	
Exeter	4 (ii)	1929	1931	Halifax	131	1931	1938	
Exeter	26	1921	1931	Plymouth	8 (ii)	1931	1938	
Exeter	27	1921	1931	Plymouth	9 (ii)	1931	1938	
Exeter	28	1925	1931	Plymouth	1 (ii)	1931	1938	
Exeter	29	1925	1931	Plymouth	2 (ii)	1931	1938	Scrapped 1942
Exeter	30	1925	1931	Plymouth	3 (ii)	1931	1938	
Exeter	31	1926	1931	Plymouth	4 (ii)	1931	1938	
Exeter	32	1926	1931	Plymouth	5 (ii)	1931	1938	Scrapped 1942
Exeter	33	1926	1931	Plymouth	6 (ii)	1931	1938	

Original fleet	Original fleet number	Entered Service	Withdrawn	Second/third fleet	Second/third fleet number	Into service	Withdrawn	Notes
Exeter	34	1926	1931	Plymouth	7 (ii)	1931	1938	
Farnworth	1-13 batch	1901/02	1906	South Lancashire Tramways	46	1906	1933	Rebuilt 1923-26
Farnworth	1-13 batch	1901/02	1906	South Lancashire Tramways	47	1906	1933	Rebuilt 1923-26; sold to Bolton
Farnworth	1-13 batch	1901/02	1906	South Lancashire Tramways	48	1906	1933	Rebuilt 1923-26; sold to Bolton
Farnworth	1-13 batch	1901/02	1906	South Lancashire Tramways	49	1906	1933	Rebuilt 1923-26
Farnworth	1-13 batch	1901/02	1906	South Lancashire Tramways	50	1906	1933	Rebuilt 1923-26; sold to Bolton
Farnworth	1-13 batch	1901/02	1906	South Lancashire Tramways	51	1906	1933	
Farnworth	1-13 batch	1901/02	1906	South Lancashire Tramways	52	1906	1933	
Farnworth	1-13 batch	1901/02	1906	South Lancashire Tramways	53	1906	1933	Rebuilt 1923-26
Farnworth	1-13 batch	1901/02	1906	South Lancashire Tramways	54	1906	1933	Rebuilt 1923-26; sold to Bolton
Farnworth	1-13 batch	1901/02	1906	South Lancashire Tramways	55	1906	1933	Rebuilt 1923-26; sold to Bolton
Farnworth	1-13 batch	1901/02	1906	South Lancashire Tramways	56	1906	1933	Rebuilt 1923-26
Farnworth	1-13 batch	1901/02	1906	South Lancashire Tramways	57	1906	1933	Rebuilt 1923-26
Farnworth	1-13 batch	1901/02	1906	South Lancashire Tramways	58	1906	1933	Rebuilt 1923-26; sold to Bolton
Gateshead	1 (ii)	1923	1951	Grimsby & Immingham	29	1951	1961	
Gateshead	3 (ii)	1923	1951	Grimsby & Immingham	24	1951	1961	
Gateshead	4 (ii)	1923	1951	Grimsby & Immingham	N/A	1951	1951	Destroyed in transit
Gateshead	5 (ii)	1927	1951	Grimsby & Immingham	20	1951	1961	
Gateshead	6 (ii)	1927	1951	Grimsby & Immingham	25	1951	1961	
Gateshead	7 (ii)	1928	1951	Grimsby & Immingham	22	1951	1961	
Gateshead	8 (ii)	1927	1951	Grimsby & Immingham	30	1951	1961	
Gateshead	9 (ii)	1927	1951	Grimsby & Immingham	19	1951	1961	
Gateshead	10 (ii)	1925	1951	Grimsby & Immingham	26	1951	1961	
Gateshead	11 (ii)	1925	1951	Grimsby & Immingham	31	1951	1961	
Gateshead	16 (ii)	1923	1951	Grimsby & Immingham	27	1951	1959	
Gateshead	17 (ii)	1925	1951	Grimsby & Immingham	DE320224	1951	1961	Used by Grimsby & Immingham as works car
Gateshead	18 (ii)	1923	1951	Grimsby & Immingham	18	1951	1961	

Gateshead	20 (ii)	1923	1951	Grimsby & Immingham	23	1951	1961	
Gateshead	56	1921	1951	Grimsby & Immingham	21	1951	1961	
Gateshead	57	1921	1951	Grimsby & Immingham	17	1951	1961	
Gateshead	58	1921	1951	Grimsby & Immingham	28	1951	1961	
Gateshead	59	1921	1951	Grimsby & Immingham	33	1951	1961	
Gateshead	60	1921	1951	Grimsby & Immingham	32	1951	1961	
Gateshead	35	1901	1911	Jarrow & District	10	1911	1961	
Glasgow	24	1901	1909	Dumbarton Burgh	27-30 batch	1909	1928	Ex-horse tram converted to electric operation
Glasgow	32	1902	1909	Dumbarton Burgh	27-30 batch	1909	1928	Ex-horse tram converted to electric operation
Glasgow	47	1902	1909	Dumbarton Burgh	27-30 batch	1909	1928	Ex-horse tram converted to electric operation
Glasgow	116	1902	1909	Dumbarton Burgh	27-30 batch	1909	1928	Ex-horse tram converted to electric operation
Glasgow	118	1903	1920	Luton	13	1923	1932	Ex-horse tram converted to electric operation 1903
Glasgow	671	1898	1921	Paisley District	N/A	1921	N/A	Body acquired for use as refreshment room at company owned tea rooms at Rouken Glen
Glasgow	666-85 batch	1898	1921	Paisley District	N/A	1921	N/A	Body acquired for use as refreshment room at company owned tea rooms at Rouken Glen
Gosport & Fareham	Unknown	1905/06	1929	Great Grimsby	1 (ii)	1930	1937	Passed to Cleethorpes UDC 1936
Gosport & Fareham	Unknown	1905/06	1929	Great Grimsby	2 (ii)	1930	1937	Passed to Cleethorpes UDC 1936
Gosport & Fareham	Unknown	1905/06	1929	Great Grimsby	3 (ii)	1930	1937	Passed to Cleethorpes UDC 1936
Gosport & Fareham	Unknown	1905/06	1929	Great Grimsby	22 (ii)	1930	1937	Passed to Cleethorpes UDC 1936
Gosport & Fareham	Unknown	1905/06	1929	Great Grimsby	23 (ii)	1930	1937	Passed to Cleethorpes UDC 1936

Original fleet	Original fleet number	Entered Service	Withdrawn	Second/third fleet	Second / third fleet number	Into service	Withdrawn	Notes
Gosport & Fareham	Unknown	1905/06	1929	Great Grimsby	24 (ii)	1930	1937	Passed to Cleethorpes UDC 1936
Gosport & Fareham	Unknown	1905/06	1929	Great Grimsby	25 (ii)	1930	1937	Passed to Cleethorpes UDC 1936
Gosport & Fareham	Unknown	1905/06	1929	Great Grimsby	26 (ii)	1930	1937	Passed to Cleethorpes UDC 1936
Gosport & Fareham	Unknown	1905/06	1929	Great Grimsby	27 (ii)	1930	1937	Passed to Cleethorpes UDC 1936
Gosport & Fareham	Unknown	1905/06	1929	Great Grimsby	28 (ii)	1930	1937	Passed to Cleethorpes UDC 1936
Gosport & Fareham	Unknown	1905/06	1929	Great Grimsby	29 (ii)	1930	1937	Passed to Cleethorpes UDC 1936
Gosport & Fareham	Unknown	1905/06	1929	Great Grimsby	30 (ii)	1930	1937	Passed to Cleethorpes UDC 1936
Gosport & Fareham	2	1905	1929	Portsdown & Horndean	2 (ii)	1930	1935	
Gosport & Fareham	8	1905	1929	Portsdown & Horndean	8 (ii)	1930	1935	
Gosport & Fareham	10	1905	1929	Portsdown & Horndean	17 (ii)	1930	1935	
Gosport & Fareham	14	1906	1929	Portsdown & Horndean	10 (ii)	1930	1935	
Gosport & Fareham	20	1906	1929	Portsdown & Horndean	14 (ii)	1930	1935	
Gosport & Fareham	21	1906	1929	Portsdown & Horndean	21	1930	1935	
Gosport & Fareham	22	1906	1929	Portsdown & Horndean	22	1930	1935	
Gravesend & Northfleet	1-10 batch	1902	1904	Jarrow & District	5 (ii)	1904	1929	Sold to South Shields
Gravesend & District	1-10 batch	1902	1904	Jarrow & District	6 (ii)	1904	1929	Sold to South Shields
Gravesend & Northfleet	1-10 batch	1902	1904	Swansea	42	1904	1937	Rebuilt 1924

Gravesend & Northfleet	1-10 batch	1902	1904	Swansea	43	1904	1937	Rebuilt 1924
Gravesend & Northfleet	1-10 batch	1902	1904	Swansea	44	1904	1937	Rebuilt 1924
Gravesend & Northfleet	1-10 batch	1902	1904	Swansea	45	1904	1937	Rebuilt 1924
Gravesend & Northfleet	1-10 batch	1902	1906	South Met	30	1906	1931	
Gravesend & Northfleet	1-10 batch	1902	1906	South Met	32	1906	1931	
Gravesend & Northfleet	1-10 batch	1902	1906	South Met	33	1906	1931	
Gravesend & Northfleet	1-10 batch	1902	1906	South Met	34	1906	1931	
Greenock & Port Glasgow	40	1908	1916	Rothesay	21	1916	1920	
Great Grimsby	35	1890	1918	Lincoln	32	1918	1921	Ex-horse tram (probably No 11 of 1890) unpowered trailer; possibly originally No 29
Great Grimsby	36	1892	1918	Lincoln	33	1918	1921	Ex-horse tram (probably No 14 of 1892) unpowered trailer; possibly originally No 30
Great Grimsby	40	1922	1925	Portsdown & Horndean	17	1925	1925	
Huddersfield	137	1931	1938	Sunderland	33 (ii)	1938	1954	
Huddersfield	138	1931	1938	Sunderland	31 (ii)	1938	1954	
Huddersfield	139	1931	1938	Sunderland	35 (ii)	1938	1954	
Huddersfield	140	1931	1938	Sunderland	34 (ii)	1938	1954	
Huddersfield	141	1931	1938	Sunderland	30 (ii)	1938	1954	
Huddersfield	142	1931	1938	Sunderland	32 (ii)	1938	1954	
Huddersfield	143	1932	1938	Sunderland	36 (ii)	1938	1954	
Huddersfield	144	1932	1938	Sunderland	29 (ii)	1938	1953	
Hull	26 (ii)	1942	1942	Leeds	449	1942	1950	

Original fleet	Original fleet number	Entered Service	Withdrawn	Second/third fleet	Second/third fleet number	Into service	Withdrawn	Notes
Hull	96	1901	1945	Leeds	6	1945	1959	Converted to single-deck snowplough 1933 and used as works car in Leeds. Preserved on withdrawal and now based at Heaton Park.
Hull	101 (ii)	1900	1916	Erith	19	1916	1933	LPTB No 19D post July 1933
Hull	104	1904	1942	Leeds	477	1943	1949	
Hull	105	1904	1945	Leeds	480	1945	1950	
Hull	109	1903	1942	Leeds	467	1942	1950	
Hull	111	1904	1945	Leeds	484	1945	1950	
Hull	113	1904	1945	Leeds	483	1945	1949	
Hull	114	1904	1942	Leeds	471	1942	1946	
Hull	115	1904	1942	Leeds	459	1942	1949	
Hull	116	1904	1942	Leeds	470	1942	1950	
Hull	117	1909	1945	Leeds	485	1946	1951	
Hull	123	1909	1945	Leeds	482	1945	1951	
Hull	124	1909	1942	Leeds	453	1942	1950	
Hull	125	1909	1942	Leeds	456	1942	1951	
Hull	126	1909	1942	Leeds	451	1942	1945	
Hull	127	1910	1942	Leeds	447	1942	1949	
Hull	128	1910	1942	Leeds	454	1942	1950	
Hull	129	1910	1942	Leeds	452	1942	1949	
Hull	130	1910	1942	Leeds	448	1942	1949	
Hull	131	1910	1942	Leeds	457	1942	1950	
Hull	132	1910	1942	Leeds	446	1942	1951	Preserved on withdrawal
Hull	133	1910	1942	Leeds	455	1942	1951	
Hull	134	1910	1942	Leeds	460	1942	1949	
Hull	135	1910	1942	Leeds	458	1942	1949	
Hull	136	1910	1942	Leeds	450	1942	1949	
Hull	138	1912	1942	Leeds	472	1942	1949	
Hull	139	1912	1945	Leeds	481	1945	1951	

Hull	140	1912	1945	Leeds	479	1945	1951	
Hull	142	1912	1945	Leeds	478	1945	1951	
Hull	147	1912	1942	Leeds	464	1942	1950	
Hull	150	1912	1942	Leeds	461	1942	1949	
Hull	152	1912	1942	Leeds	469	1942	1949	
Hull	153	1912	1942	Leeds	463	1942	1949	
Hull	154	1912	1942	Leeds	473	1942	1949	
Hull	155	1912	1942	Leeds	466	1942	1949	
Hull	156	1912	1942	Leeds	465	1942	1950	
Hull	158	1912	1945	Leeds	476	1943	1946	
Hull	159	1912	1942	Leeds	462	1942	1950	
Hull	160	1912	1945	Leeds	486	1945	1951	
Hull	163	1915	1942	Leeds	474	1942	1950	
Hull	164	1915	1942	Leeds	475	1942	1949	
Hull	173	1915	1945	Leeds	487	1945	1950	
Hull	174	1915	1942	Leeds	468	1942	1949	
Ilkeston/Notts & Derby	1-9 batch	1902	1920	Carlisle	13 (ii)	1920	1931	
Ilkeston/Notts & Derby	10-13 batch	1903	1920	Carlisle	14 (ii)	1925	1931	Carlisle No 14 (ii) had new EE body on used – probably ex-Ilkeston – truck
Ilkeston/Notts & Derby	1-9 batch	1902	1920	Carlisle	15 (ii)	1923	1931	Carlisle No 15 (ii) had new EE body on used – probably ex-Ilkeston – truck
Ilkeston/Notts & Derby	1-9 batch	1902	1919	Dunfermline	44	1919	By 1925	
Ilkeston/Notts & Derby	1-9 batch	1902	1919	Dunfermline	45	1919	By 1925	
Ipswich	1-36 batch	1903	1925	Scarborough	21 (ii)	1925	1931	Body from an ex-Ipswich car placed on truck of original Scarborough No 21, which had been scrapped following an accident.
Ipswich	1-36 batch	1903	1925	Scarborough	23	1925	1931	

Original fleet	Original fleet number	Entered Service	Withdrawn	Second/third fleet	Second / third fleet number	Into service	Withdrawn	Notes
Ipswich	1-36 batch	1903	1925	Scarborough	24	1925	1931	
Ipswich	1-36 batch	1903	1925	Scarborough	25	1925	1931	
Ipswich	1-36 batch	1903	1925	Scarborough	26	1925	1931	
Ipswich	1-36 batch	1903	1925	Scarborough	27	1925	1931	
Ipswich	1-36 batch	1903	1925	Scarborough	28	1925	1931	
Jarrow & District	5 (i)	1906	1908	Gravesend & District	5 (ii)	1908	1929	
Jarrow & District	6 (i)	1906	1908	Gravesend & District	6 (ii)	1908	1929	
Jarrow & District	5 (ii)	1907	1929	South Shields	48	1930	1935	Ex- Gravesend & District
Jarrow & District	6 (ii)	1907	1929	South Shields	29 (ii)	1930	1935	Ex- Gravesend & District
Kirkcaldy	Unknown	1902-16	1931	Wemyss & District	22	1931	1932	See caption on page 84 for details
Kirkcaldy	Unknown	1902-16	1931	Wemyss & District	23	1931	1932	
Kirkcaldy	Unknown	1902-16	1931	Wemyss & District	24	1931	1932	
Kirkcaldy	Unknown	1902-16	1931	Wemyss & District	25	1931	1932	
Kirkcaldy	Unknown	1902-16	1931	Wemyss & District	26	1931	1932	
Kirkcaldy	Unknown	1902-16	1931	Wemyss & District	27	1931	1932	
Kirkcaldy	Unknown	1902-16	1931	Wemyss & District	28	1931	1932	
Kirkcaldy	Unknown	1902-16	1931	Wemyss & District	29	1931	1932	
LCC	102-201 batch	1903	1917	Newport	45	1917	By 1937	Class B car
LCC	102-201 batch	1903	1917	Newport	46	1917	By 1937	Class B car
LCC	102-201 batch	1903	1917	Newport	47	1917	By 1937	Class B car
LCC	102-201 batch	1903	1917	Newport	48	1917	By 1937	Class B car
LCC	102-201 batch	1903	1917	Newport	49	1917	By 1937	Class B car
LCC	102-201 batch	1903	1917	Newport	50	1917	By 1937	Class B car
LCC	102-201 batch	1903	1917	Rotherham	50	1917	1926	Class B car; renumbered 39 (ii) in 1922

LCC	102–201 batch	1903	1917	Rotherham	51	1917	1926	Class B car; renumbered 40 (ii) in 1922; sold to Sheffield in 1926
LCC	102–201 batch	1903	1917	Rotherham	52	1917	1926	Class B car; renumbered 41 (ii) in 1922; sold to Sheffield in 1926
LCC	102–201 batch	1903	1917	Rotherham	53	1917	1926	Class B car; renumbered 42 (ii) in 1922; sold to Sheffield in 1926
LCC	102–201 batch	1903	1917	Rotherham	54	1917	1926	Class B car; renumbered 43 (ii) in 1922; sold to Sheffield in 1926
LCC	102–201 batch	1903	1917	Rotherham	55	1917	1926	Class B car; renumbered 44 (ii) in 1922; sold to Sheffield in 1926
LCC	102–201 batch	1903	1917	Rotherham	56	1917	1926	Class B car; renumbered 45 (ii) in 1922; sold to Sheffield in 1926
LCC	102–201 batch	1903	1917	Rotherham	57	1917	1926	Class B car; renumbered 46 in 1922; sold to Sheffield in 1926
LCC	102–201 batch	1903	1917	Rotherham	58	1917	1926	Class B car; renumbered 47 (ii) in 1922; sold to Sheffield in 1926
LCC	102–201 batch	1903	1917	Rotherham	59	1917	1926	Class B car; renumbered 48 (ii) in 1922
LCC	102–201 batch	1903	1915	Bexley	17	1915	1919	Class B car
LCC	102–201 batch	1903	1915	Bexley	18	1915	1919	Class B car
LCC	102–201 batch	1903	1915	Bexley	19	1915	1919	Class B car

Original fleet	Original fleet number	Entered Service	Withdrawn	Second/third fleet	Second / third fleet number	Into service	Withdrawn	Notes
LCC	102-201 batch	1903	1915	Bexley	20	1915	1919	Class B car
LCC	102-201 batch	1903	1915	Bexley	21	1915	1933	Class B car
LCC	102-201 batch	1903	1915	Bexley	22	1915	1919	Class B car
LCC	102-201 batch	1903	1915	Bexley	23	1915	1933	Class B car
LCC	102-201 batch	1903	1917	Bexley	24	1917	1933	Class B car
LCC	102-201 batch	1903	1917	Bexley	25	1917	1933	Class B car
LCC	102-201 batch	1903	1917	Bexley	26	1917	1920	Class B car
LCC	102-201 batch	1903	1917	Bexley	27	1917	1933	Class B car
LCC	102-201 batch	1903	1918	Bexley	28	1918	1933	Class B car
LCC	102-201 batch	1903	1918	Bexley	29	1918	1933	Class B car
LCC	102-201 batch	1903	1918	Bexley	30	1918	1933	Class B car
LCC	102-201 batch	1903	1918	Bexley	31	1918	1933	Class B car
LCC	102-201 batch	1903	1918	Bexley	32	1918	1933	Class B car
LCC	102-201 batch	1903	1918	Bexley	33	1918	1933	Class B car
LCC	102-201 batch	1903	1918	Bexley	34	1918	1933	Class B car
LCC	102-201 batch	1903	1918	Bexley	35	1918	1933	Class B car
LCC	102-201 batch	1903	1918	Bexley	36	1918	1933	Class B car
LCC	102-201 batch	1903	1918	Bexley	37	1918	1933	Class B car

LCC	102–201 batch	1903	1918	Bexley	38	1918	1933	Class B car
LCC	102–201 batch	1903	1918	Bexley	39	1918	1933	Class B car
LCC	103	1903	1917	Sheffield	363	1917	1926–31 period	Class B car
LCC	108	1903	1917	Sheffield	362	1917	1926–31 period	Class B car
LCC	116	1903	1917	Sheffield	357	1917	1926–31 period	Class B car
LCC	119	1903	1917	Sheffield	358	1917	1926–31 period	Class B car
LCC	121	1903	1917	Sheffield	360	1917	1926–31 period	Class B car
LCC	126	1903	1917	Sheffield	359	1917	1926–31 period	Class B car; cut down to single deck by the LCC
LCC	135	1903	1918	Southampton	75	1918	1934	Class B car
LCC	149	1903	1918	Sheffield	207 (ii)	1918	1926–31 period	Class B car
LCC	152	1903	1917	Sheffield	364	1917	1926–31 period	Class B car
LCC	154	1903	1918	Southampton	76	1918	1948	Class B car
LCC	156	1903	1917	Sheffield	361	1917	1926–31 period	Class B car
LCC	160	1903	1917	Sheffield	356	1917	1926–31 period	Class B car
LCC	161	1903	1918	Southampton	77	1918	1947	Class B car
LCC	166	1903	1918	Sheffield	125 (ii)	1918	1926–31 period	Class B car; retrucked to Peckham P22 by Sheffield
LCC	170	1903	1918	Sheffield	187 (ii)	1918	1926–31 period	Class B car
LCC	171	1903	1918	Sheffield	203 (ii)	1918	1926–31 period	Class B car
LCC	173	1903	1918	Sheffield	56 (ii)	1918	1926–31 period	Class B car; retrucked to Peckham P22 by Sheffield; renumbered 128 in 1924

Original fleet	Original fleet number	Entered Service	Withdrawn	Second/third fleet	Second / third fleet number	Into service	Withdrawn	Notes
LCC	179	1903	1918	Sheffield	209 (ii)	1918	1926-31 period	Class B car
LCC	181	1903	1918	Sheffield	129 (ii)	1918	1926-31 period	Class B car; retrucked to Peckham P22 by Sheffield
LCC	185	1903	1918	Sheffield	210 (ii)	1918	1926-31 period	Class B car
LCC	186	1903	1918	Sheffield	188	1918	1926-31 period	Class B car
LCC	188	1903	1917	Sheffield	365 (ii)	1917	1926-31 period	Class B car
LCC	192	1903	1918	Southampton	78	1918	1948	Class B car
LCC	193	1903	1918	Sheffield	94 (ii)	1918	1926-31 period	Class B car; retrucked to Peckham P22 by Sheffield; renumbered 90 in 1925
LCC	198	1903	1918	Southampton	79	1918	1948	Class B car
LCC	200	1903	1918	Southampton	80	1918	1948	Class B car
Leamington & Warwick	11	1901	1930	Llandudno & Colwyn Bay	23	1930	1936	Ex-Taunton; cut down to single-deck for use as works car by Leamington & Warwick
Leeds	143-54 batch	1899	1899	Swansea	31	1899	By 1929	
Leeds	143-54 batch	1899	1899	Swansea	32	1899	By 1929	
Leeds	143-54 batch	1899	1899	Swansea	33	1899	By 1929	
Leeds	143-54 batch	1899	1899	Swansea	34	1899	By 1933	Renumbered 40 after rebuilding with fully-enclosed top deck
Leeds	143-54 batch	1899	1899	Swansea	35	1899	By 1933	
Leeds	143-54 batch	1899	1899	Swansea	36	1899	By 1933	
Leeds	143-54 batch	1899	1899	Swansea	37	1899	By 1933	
Leeds	143-54 batch	1899	1899	Swansea	38	1899	By 1933	
Leeds	143-54 batch	1899	1899	Swansea	39	1899	By 1933	
Leeds	143-54 batch	1899	1899	Swansea	40	1899	By 1933	

Leeds	143-54 batch	1899	1899	Swansea	41	1899	By 1933	Originally hired and then bought outright
Leeds	125A	1908	1942	Rotherham	14	1942	1949	
Leeds	133	1899	1919	West Riding	68	1919	Between 1925 and 1932	Probable number
Leeds	138	1899	1919	West Riding	69	1919	Between 1925 and 1932	Probable number
Leeds	147	1899	1919	West Riding	70	1919	1932	Probable number
Leeds	148	1899	1919	West Riding	71	1919	Between 1925 and 1932	Probable number
Leeds	163	1899	1919	West Riding	72	1919	Between 1925 and 1932	Probable number
Leeds	170	1899	1919	West Riding	73	1919	Between 1925 and 1932	Probable number
Leeds	177	1899	1919	West Riding	74	1919	1932	Probable number
Leeds	180	1899	1919	West Riding	75	1919	Between 1925 and 1932	Probable number
Lincoln	9	1919	1929	Preston	13 (ii)	1929	1935	
Lincoln	10	1919	1929	Preston	18 (ii)	1929	1935	
Lincoln	11	1919	1929	Preston	22 (ii)	1929	1935	
Liverpool	48	1899	1921	Gateshead	29 (ii)	1921	1950	Originally Liverpool 479; renumbered 1900
Liverpool	49 or 50	1899	1921	Gateshead	30 (ii)	1921	1950	Originally Liverpool 480 or 481; renumbered 1900
Liverpool	49 or 50	1899	1921	Gateshead	38 (ii)	1921	1950	Originally Liverpool 480 or 481; renumbered 1900
Liverpool	464-68 batch	1899	1899	Leeds	44	1900	1927	Rejected by Liverpool; top cover fitted 1910
Liverpool	464-68 batch	1899	1899	Leeds	46	1900	1927	Rejected by Liverpool; top cover fitted 1910
Liverpool	464-68 batch	1899	1899	Leeds	55	1900	1927	Rejected by Liverpool; top cover fitted 1910

Original fleet	Original fleet number	Entered Service	Withdrawn	Second/third fleet	Second / third fleet number	Into service	Withdrawn	Notes
Liverpool	464-68 batch	1899	1899	Leeds	79	1900	1926	Rejected by Liverpool; top cover fitted 1910
Liverpool	464-68 batch	1899	1899	Leeds	83	1900	1922	Rejected by Liverpool; top cover fitted 1910
Liverpool	869	1936	1954	Glasgow	1055 (ii)	1955	1960	Preserved on withdrawal; now based at NTM
Liverpool	871	1936	1954	Glasgow	1047 (ii)	1955	1959	
Liverpool	874	1936	1954	Glasgow	1044 (ii)	1955	1959	
Liverpool	875	1936	1954	Glasgow	1046 (ii)	1955	1958	
Liverpool	877	1936	1954	Glasgow	1045 (ii)	1955	1959	
Liverpool	878	1936	1954	Glasgow	1041 (ii)	1955	1959	
Liverpool	880	1936	1954	Glasgow	1037 (ii)	1955	1959	
Liverpool	881	1936	1954	Glasgow	1033 (ii)	1954	1960	
Liverpool	883	1936	1954	Glasgow	1038 (ii)	1955	1959	
Liverpool	884	1936	1954	Glasgow	1053 (ii)	1955	1959	
Liverpool	885	1936	1954	Glasgow	1034 (ii)	1955	1959	
Liverpool	886	1936	1954	Glasgow	1042 (ii)	1955	1957	
Liverpool	887	1936	1954	Glasgow	1048 (ii)	1955	1959	
Liverpool	890	1936	1954	Glasgow	1054 (ii)	1955	1959	
Liverpool	891	1936	1954	Glasgow	1036 (ii)	1955	1960	
Liverpool	893	1936	1954	Glasgow	1049 (ii)	1955	1959	
Liverpool	897	1936	1954	Glasgow	1052 (ii)	1955	1959	
Liverpool	899	1936	1954	Glasgow	1031 (ii)	1954	1960	
Liverpool	901	1936	1954	Glasgow	1032 (ii)	1954	1960	
Liverpool	902	1936	1954	Glasgow	1035 (ii)	1955	1959	
Liverpool	903	1936	1954	Glasgow	1043 (ii)	1955	1959	
Liverpool	904	1936	1954	Glasgow	1056 (ii)	1956	1959	
Liverpool	918	1936	1953	Glasgow	1022 (ii)	1954	1959	
Liverpool	919	1936	1953	Glasgow	1030 (ii)	1954	1960	
Liverpool	921	1936	1953	Glasgow	1016 (ii)	1953	1960	
Liverpool	922	1936	1953	Glasgow	1018 (ii)	1953	1959	
Liverpool	923	1936	1953	Glasgow	1012 (ii)	1953	1960	

Operator	Number			Location	ID			Notes
Liverpool	924	1936	1953	Glasgow	1027 (ii)	1954	1959	
Liverpool	925	1936	1953	Glasgow	1025 (ii)	1954	1960	
Liverpool	926	1936	1953	Glasgow	1019 (ii)	1954	1959	
Liverpool	927	1936	1953	Glasgow	1024 (ii)	1954	1958	
Liverpool	928	1936	1953	Glasgow	1013 (ii)	1953	1959	
Liverpool	929	1936	1953	Glasgow	1029 (ii)	1954	1959	
Liverpool	930	1936	1953	Glasgow	1010 (ii)	1953	1959	
Liverpool	931	1936	1953	Glasgow	1011 (ii)	1953	1959	
Liverpool	932	1936	1953	Glasgow	1014 (ii)	1953	1959	
Liverpool	933	1936	1953	Glasgow	1028 (ii)	1954	1959	
Liverpool	934	1936	1953	Glasgow	1007 (ii)	1953	1959	
Liverpool	935	1936	1953	Glasgow	1009 (ii)	1953	1959	
Liverpool	936	1936	1953	Glasgow	1021 (ii)	1954	1960	
Liverpool	937	1936	1953	Glasgow	1020 (ii)	1953	1958	
Liverpool	938	1936	1953	Glasgow	1008 (ii)	1953	1959	
Liverpool	939	1936	1953	Glasgow	1023 (ii)	1954	1959	
Liverpool	940	1936	1953	Glasgow	1015 (ii)	1953	1959	
Liverpool	941	1937	1953	Glasgow	1026 (ii)	1954	1959	
Liverpool	942	1937	1953	Glasgow	1006 (ii)	1953	1959	
London Transport	1	1932	1951	Leeds	301 (ii)	1951	1957	Preserved at the NTM
London Transport	33	1932	1938	Sunderland	2 (ii)	1938	1954	Ex-Ilford Corporation
London Transport	34	1932	1938	Sunderland	3 (ii)	1938	1954	Ex-Ilford Corporation
London Transport	35	1932	1938	Sunderland	4 (ii)	1938	1954	Ex-Ilford Corporation
London Transport	36	1932	1938	Sunderland	5 (ii)	1938	1954	Ex-Ilford Corporation
London Transport	37	1932	1938	Sunderland	6 (ii)	1938	1954	Ex-Ilford Corporation
London Transport	38	1932	1937	Sunderland	7 (ii)	1937	1954	Ex-Ilford Corporation
London Transport	39	1932	1938	Sunderland	8 (ii)	1938	1954	Ex-Ilford Corporation
London Transport	40	1932	1938	Sunderland	9 (ii)	1938	1954	Ex-Ilford Corporation

Original fleet	Original fleet number	Entered Service	Withdrawn	Second/third fleet	Second / third fleet number	Into service	Withdrawn	Notes
London Transport	1881	1930	1939	Leeds	277 (ii)	1939	1956	'HR/2' class
London Transport	1883	1930	1939	Leeds	278 (ii)	1939	1957	'HR/2' class
London Transport	1886	1930	1939	Leeds	279 (ii)	1939	1957	'HR/2' class
London Transport	2066	1931	1950	Leeds	506	1950	1959	'Feltham'
London Transport	2068	1931	1951	Leeds	539	1951	1959	'Feltham'
London Transport	2069	1931	1950	Leeds	505	1950	1957	'Feltham'
London Transport	2070	1931	1950	Leeds	507	1950	1953	'Feltham'
London Transport	2071	1931	1950	Leeds	530	1951	1957	'Feltham'
London Transport	2072	1931	1950	Leeds	521	1951	1959	'Feltham'
London Transport	2073	1931	1950	Leeds	508	1951	1956	'Feltham'
London Transport	2074	1931	1950	Leeds	510	1950	1959	'Feltham'
London Transport	2075	1931	1950	Leeds	527	1951	1957	'Feltham'
London Transport	2076	1931	1950	Leeds	524	1951	1958	'Feltham'
London Transport	2077	1931	1950	Leeds	503	1950	1957	'Feltham'
London Transport	2078	1931	1950	Leeds	509	1950	1958	'Feltham'
London Transport	2079	1931	1951	Leeds	550	1951	1957	'Feltham'
London Transport	2080	1931	1950	Leeds	516	1951	1957	'Feltham'
London Transport	2081	1931	1950	Leeds	520	1951	1959	'Feltham'

London Transport	2082	1931	1950	Leeds	504	1950	1959	'Feltham'
London Transport	2083	1931	1950	Leeds	515	1951	1959	'Feltham'
London Transport	2084	1931	1950	Leeds	519	1951	1959	'Feltham'
London Transport	2085	1931	1950	Leeds	526	1951	1959	'Feltham'; preserved in the USA
London Transport	2086	1931	1950	Leeds	528	1951	1957	'Feltham'
London Transport	2087	1931	1950	Leeds	518	1951	1959	'Feltham'
London Transport	2088	1931	1950	Leeds	512	1951	1959	'Feltham'
London Transport	2089	1931	1951	Leeds	537	1951	1957	'Feltham'
London Transport	2090	1931	1951	Leeds	544	1951	1956	'Feltham'
London Transport	2092	1931	1951	Leeds	533	1951	1957	'Feltham'
London Transport	2093	1931	1950	Leeds	515	1951	1959	'Feltham'
London Transport	2094	1931	1951	Leeds	538	1951	1959	'Feltham'
London Transport	2095	1931	1951	Leeds	543	1951	1957	'Feltham'
London Transport	2096	1931	1950	Leeds	523	1951	1959	'Feltham'
London Transport	2097	1931	1950	Leeds	502	1950	1959	'Feltham'
London Transport	2098	1931	1951	Leeds	542	1951	1959	'Feltham'
London Transport	2099	1931	1949	Leeds	501	1949	1959	'Feltham'; initially operated as No 2099 in Leeds before renumbering; preserved
London Transport	2100	1931	1950	Leeds	513	1950	1957	'Feltham'

Original fleet	Original fleet number	Entered Service	Withdrawn	Second/third fleet	Second / third fleet number	Into service	Withdrawn	Notes
London Transport	2101	1931	1951	Leeds	546	1951	1959	'Feltham'
London Transport	2102	1931	1951	Leeds	534	1951	1959	'Feltham'
London Transport	2103	1931	1951	Leeds	548	1951	1957	'Feltham'
London Transport	2104	1931	1951	Leeds	532	1951	1959	'Feltham'
London Transport	2105	1931	1950	Leeds	511	1950	1957	'Feltham'
London Transport	2106	1931	1951	Leeds	531	1951	1959	'Feltham'
London Transport	2107	1931	1951	Leeds	541	1951	1956	'Feltham'
London Transport	2108	1931	1950	Leeds	522	1951	1958	'Feltham'
London Transport	2110	1931	1951	Leeds	536	1951	1958	'Feltham'
London Transport	2111	1931	1951	Leeds	545	1951	1957	'Feltham'
London Transport	2112	1931	1951	Leeds	547	1951	1957	'Feltham'
London Transport	2114	1931	1951	Leeds	540	1951	1957	'Feltham'
London Transport	2115	1931	1950	Leeds	514	1951	1959	'Feltham'
London Transport	2116	1931	1950	Leeds	529	1951	1959	'Feltham'
London Transport	2117	1931	1951	Leeds	549	1951	1959	'Feltham'
London Transport	2118	1931	1950	Leeds	517	1951	1959	'Feltham'
London Transport	2119	1931	1951	Leeds	535	1951	1959	'Feltham'
London Transport	2120	1931	1951	Leeds	557	1951	1959	'Feltham'

London Transport		1931	1951		Leeds		1951	1957	'Feltham'
London Transport	2121	1931	1951		Leeds	558	1951	1957	'Feltham'
London Transport	2123	1931	1951		Leeds	564	1955	1959	'Feltham'
London Transport	2124	1931	1951		Leeds	573	1956	1959	'Feltham'
London Transport	2125	1931	1951		Leeds	561	1952	1959	'Feltham'
London Transport	2126	1931	1951		Leeds	565	1955	1959	'Feltham'
London Transport	2127	1931	1951		Leeds	568	1956	1959	'Feltham'
London Transport	2128	1931	1951		Leeds	(572)	Never	1956	'Feltham'; scrapped without entering service in Leeds
London Transport	2129	1931	1951		Leeds	574	1956	1959	'Feltham'
London Transport	2131	1931	1951		Leeds	555	1951	1956	'Feltham'
London Transport	2132	1931	1951		Leeds	569	1955	1959	'Feltham'
London Transport	2133	1931	1951		Leeds	582	1956	1959	'Feltham'
London Transport	2134	1931	1951		Leeds	566	1955	1957	'Feltham'
London Transport	2135	1931	1951		Leeds	(584)	Never	1956	'Feltham'; scrapped without entering service in Leeds
London Transport	2136	1931	1951		Leeds	567	1955	1957	'Feltham'
London Transport	2137	1931	1951		Leeds	559	1952	1957	'Feltham'
London Transport	2138	1931	1951		Leeds	554	1951	1959	'Feltham'
London Transport	2139	1931	1951		Leeds	551	1951	1956	'Feltham'
London Transport	2140	1931	1951		Leeds	563	1955	1957	'Feltham'
London Transport	2141	1931	1951		Leeds	570	1955	1957	'Feltham'

Original fleet	Original fleet number	Entered Service	Withdrawn	Second/third fleet	Second / third fleet number	Into service	Withdrawn	Notes
London Transport	2142	1931	1951	Leeds	(578)	Never	1956	'Feltham'; scrapped without entering service in Leeds
London Transport	2143	1931	1951	Leeds	581	1952	1958	'Feltham'
London Transport	2145	1931	1951	Leeds	(577)	Never	1956	'Feltham'; scrapped without entering service in Leeds
London Transport	2146	1931	1951	Leeds	579	1952	1956	'Feltham'
London Transport	2147	1931	1951	Leeds	587	1955	1959	'Feltham'
London Transport	2148	1931	1951	Leeds	560	1952	1957	'Feltham'
London Transport	2149	1931	1951	Leeds	580	1955	1956	'Feltham'
London Transport	2150	1931	1951	Leeds	553	1951	1957	'Feltham'
London Transport	2151	1931	1951	Leeds	(576)	Never	1956	'Feltham'; scrapped without entering service in Leeds
London Transport	2152	1931	1951	Leeds	556	1951	1959	'Feltham'
London Transport	2153	1931	1951	Leeds	588	1952	1952	'Feltham'
London Transport	2154	1931	1951	Leeds	589	1955	1959	'Feltham'
London Transport	2155	1931	1951	Leeds	(571)	Never	1956	'Feltham'; scrapped without entering service in Leeds
London Transport	2156	1931	1951	Leeds	(575)	Never	1956	'Feltham'; scrapped without entering service in Leeds
London Transport	2157	1931	1951	Leeds	586	1952	1957	'Feltham'
London Transport	2158	1931	1951	Leeds	590	1952	1957	'Feltham'

Operator	Number	Year	Year	Location	Number	Year	Year	Type
London Transport	2159	1931	1951	Leeds	585	1956	1959	'Feltham'
London Transport	2160	1931	1951	Leeds	583	1952	1957	'Feltham'
London Transport	2161	1931	1951	Leeds	562	1951	1956	'Feltham'
London Transport	2164	1931	1950	Leeds	552	1951	1956	'Feltham'
London United	108	1901	1919	Blackpool	93-98 batch	1919	1934	
London United	118	1901	1919	Blackpool	93-98 batch	1919	1934	
London United	125	1901	1919	Blackpool	93-98 batch	1919	1934	
London United	137	1901	1919	Blackpool	93-98 batch	1919	1934	
London United	149	1901	1919	Blackpool	93-98 batch	1919	1934	
London United	150	1901	1919	Blackpool	93-98 batch	1919	1934	
London United	151-300 batch	1902	1916	Ilford	15 (ii)	1916	1933	LUT Class W
London United	151-300 batch	1902	1916	Ilford	16 (ii)	1916	1933	LUT Class W
London United	151-300 batch	1902	1916	Ilford	17	1916	1933	LUT Class W
London United	151-300 batch	1902	1916	Ilford	18	1916	1933	LUT Class W
London United	151-300 batch	1902	1919	Walthamstow	47	1919	1930	LUT Class W
London United	151-300 batch	1902	1919	Walthamstow	48	1919	1930	LUT Class W
London United	151-300 batch	1902	1919	Walthamstow	49	1919	1932	LUT Class W
London United	151-300 batch	1902	1919	Walthamstow	50	1919	1932	LUT Class W
London United	151-300 batch	1902	1919	Walthamstow	51	1919	1932	LUT Class W
London United	151-300 batch	1902	1919	Walthamstow	52	1919	1932	LUT Class W
Manchester	104	1931	1948	Leeds	281 (ii)	1948	1954	'Pilcher' car
Manchester	106	1930	1948	Aberdeen	49 (ii)	1948	1956	'Pilcher' car
Manchester	121	1930	1947	Aberdeen	39 (ii)	1948	1955	'Pilcher' car
Manchester	125	1931	1947	Edinburgh	404	1947	1954	'Pilcher' car
Manchester	131	1930	1947	Sunderland	42 (ii)	1947	1954	'Pilcher' car
Manchester	141	1930	1948	Aberdeen	47 (ii)	1948	1955	'Pilcher' car

Original fleet	Original fleet number	Entered Service	Withdrawn	Second/third fleet	Second / third fleet number	Into service	Withdrawn	Notes
Manchester	144	1932	1948	Leeds	284 (ii)	1949	1951	'Pilcher' car
Manchester	161	1931	1947	Aberdeen	42 (ii)	1948	1955	'Pilcher' car
Manchester	163	1930	1947	Sunderland	39 (ii)	1947	1953	'Pilcher' car
Manchester	173	1931	1946	Edinburgh	401	1947	1954	'Pilcher' car
Manchester	176	1931	1947	Sunderland	40 (ii)	1947	1953	'Pilcher' car
Manchester	196	1931	1947	Edinburgh	403	1947	1954	'Pilcher' car
Manchester	217	1931	1948	Edinburgh	406	1948	1954	'Pilcher' car
Manchester	225	1932	1948	Aberdeen	50 (ii)	1948	1955	'Pilcher' car
Manchester	228	1931	1947	Sunderland	37 (ii)	1947	1954	'Pilcher' car
Manchester	231	1932	1948	Edinburgh	408	1949	1954	'Pilcher' car
Manchester	242	1930	1948	Edinburgh	409	1949	1954	'Pilcher' car
Manchester	263	1931	1948	Leeds	285 (ii)	1948	1953	'Pilcher' car
Manchester	266	1930	1948	Leeds	283 (ii)	1948	1953	'Pilcher' car
Manchester	270	1930	1948	Aberdeen	48 (ii)	1948	1955	'Pilcher' car
Manchester	272	1931	1948	Leeds	282 (ii)	1948	1952	'Pilcher' car
Manchester	274	1931	1948	Aberdeen	45 (ii)	198	1956	'Pilcher' car
Manchester	287	1931	1946	Leeds	287 (ii)	1946	1953	'Pilcher' car; renumbered 280 (ii)
Manchester	349	1930	1948	Edinburgh	410	1949	1954	'Pilcher' car
Manchester	370	1931	1948	Leeds	286 (ii)	1949	1954	'Pilcher' car
Manchester	380	1931	1947	Sunderland	41 (ii)	1947	1954	'Pilcher' car
Manchester	381	1930	1948	Edinburgh	411	1949	1954	'Pilcher' car
Manchester	389	1930	1948	Edinburgh	407	1948	1954	'Pilcher' car
Manchester	420	1931	1947	Aberdeen	41 (ii)	1948	1955	'Pilcher' car
Manchester	493	1931	1948	Aberdeen	40 (ii)	1948	1955	'Pilcher' car
Manchester	502	1930	1948	Aberdeen	52 (ii)	1948	1955	'Pilcher' car
Manchester	503	1931	1947	Sunderland	38 (ii)	1947	1954	'Pilcher' car
Manchester	510	1932	1948	Aberdeen	51 (ii)	1948	1955	'Pilcher' car
Manchester	558	1932	1948	Edinburgh	405	1948	1954	'Pilcher' car
Manchester	610	1931	1947	Aberdeen	44 (ii)	1948	1955	'Pilcher' car
Manchester	669	1932	1948	Aberdeen	46 (ii)	1948	1955	'Pilcher' car
Manchester	671	1931	1947	Aberdeen	42 (ii)	1948	1955	'Pilcher' car
Manchester	676	1932	1946	Edinburgh	402	1947	1954	'Pilcher' car
Mansfield & District	23	1912	1918	Llanelly	15 (?)	1918	1920	Returned to Mansfield

Mansfield & District	24	1912	1918	Llanelly	16 (?)	1918	1920	Returned to Mansfield
Mansfield & District	27	1925	1932	Sunderland	21 (ii)	1933	1953	Body only
Mansfield & District	28	1925	1932	Sunderland	24 (ii)	1933	1954	Body only
MET/LPTB	331/2168	1930	1937	Sunderland	100	1937	1951	Preserved on withdrawal; now based at NTM
Mexborough & Swinton	7	1906	1928	Dewsbury & Ossett	11	1928	1933	Sold as balcony top with replacement Brill 21E truck
Mexborough & Swinton	10	1906	1911	Dewsbury & Ossett	10	1911	1933	Sold as open-top car; top cover fitted 1922; replacement 21E truck also fitted
Mexborough & Swinton	14	1906	1911	Dewsbury & Ossett	9	1911	1933	Sold as open-top car; top cover fitted 1922; replacement 21E truck also fitted
Mexborough & Swinton	15	1906	1928	Dewsbury & Ossett	12	1928	1933	Sold as balcony top with replacement Brill 21E truck
Middlesbrough	132–40 batch	1921	1934	Southend-on-Sea	62	1934	1939	
Middlesbrough	132–40 batch	1921	1934	Southend-on-Sea	63	1934	1939	
Middlesbrough	132–40 batch	1921	1934	Southend-on-Sea	64	1934	1939	
Middlesbrough	132–40 batch	1921	1934	Southend-on-Sea	65	1934	1942	
Middleton	1-10 batch	1901	1925	Manchester	994	1925	1930	
Middleton	1-10 batch	1901	1925	Manchester	995	1925	1930	
Middleton	1-10 batch	1901	1925	Manchester	996	1925	1930	
Middleton	1-10 batch	1901	1925	Manchester	997	1925	By 1939	
Middleton	1-10 batch	1901	1925	Manchester	998	1925	1930	
Middleton	1-10 batch	1901	1925	Manchester	999	1925	1930	
Middleton	1-10 batch	1901	1925	Manchester	529	1925	1937	Latterly used as sand car
Middleton	1-10 batch	1901	1925	Manchester	(1001)	1925	1925	
Middleton	1-10 batch	1901	1925	Manchester	(1002)	1925	1925	
Middleton	1-10 batch	1901	1925	Manchester	(1003)	1925	1925	

Original fleet	Original fleet number	Entered Service	Withdrawn	Second/third fleet	Second / third fleet number	Into service	Withdrawn	Notes
Middleton	11 (ii)	1905	1925	Rochdale	2 (ii)	1925	By 1931	
Middleton	12 (ii)	1905	1925	Rochdale	12 (ii)	1925	By 1931	
Middleton	13 (ii)	1905	1925	Rochdale	13 (ii)	1925	By 1931	
Middleton	14 (ii)	1905	1925	Rochdale	14 (ii)	1925	By 1931	
Middleton	15 (ii)	1905	1925	Rochdale	15 (ii)	1925	By 1931	
Middleton	11-20 batch	1901	1904	Oldham, Ashton & Hyde	27	1904	1928	Transferred in 1921 to Ashton-under-Lyne Corporation as No 39
Middleton	11-20 batch	1901	1904	Oldham, Ashton & Hyde	28	1904	1928	Transferred in 1921 to Ashton-under-Lyne Corporation as No 40
Middleton	11-20 batch	1901	1904	Oldham, Ashton & Hyde	29	1904	By 1927	Transferred in 1921 to Hyde Corporation and then to SHMD as No 29
Middleton	11-20 batch	1901	1904	Oldham, Ashton & Hyde	30	1904	By 1927	Transferred in 1921 to Hyde Corporation and then to SHMD as No 30
Middleton	11-20 batch	1901	1905	Swansea	50	1905	By 1923	
Middleton	11-20 batch	1901	1905	Swansea	51	1905	By 1923	
Middleton	11-20 batch	1901	1905	Swansea	52	1905	By 1923	
Middleton	11-20 batch	1901	1905	Swansea	53	1905	By 1923	
Middleton	11-20 batch	1901	1905	Swansea	54	1905	By 1923	
Middleton	11-20 batch	1901	1905	Swansea	55	1905	By 1923	
Middleton	21	1902	1925	South Lancashire Tramways		1925	1933	
Middleton	22-25 batch	1902	1916-1920	Potteries	99 (ii)	1916-1920	1928	
Middleton	22-25 batch	1902	1916-1920	Potteries	100 (ii)	1916-1920	1928	
Middleton	22-25 batch	1902	1916-1920	Potteries	119	1916-1920	1928	
Middleton	22-25 batch	1902	1916-1920	Potteries	120	1916-1920	1928	

Middleton	27-34 batch	1903	1925	Oldham	113	1925	1935	Ex-Oldham, Ashton & Hyde; retrucked with Brill 21E
Middleton	27-34 batch	1903	1925	Oldham	114	1925	1935	Ex-Oldham, Ashton & Hyde; retrucked with Brill 21E
Middleton	27-34 batch	1903	1925	Oldham	115	1925	1935	Ex-Oldham, Ashton & Hyde; retrucked with Brill 21E
Middleton	27-34 batch	1903	1925	Oldham	116	1925	1935	Ex-Oldham, Ashton & Hyde; retrucked with Brill 21E
Middleton	27-34 batch	1903	1925	Oldham	117	1925	1934	Ex-Oldham, Ashton & Hyde; retrucked with Brill 21E
Middleton	27-34 batch	1903	1925	Oldham	118	1925	1935	Ex-Oldham, Ashton & Hyde; retrucked with Brill 21E
Middleton	27-34 batch	1903	1925	Oldham	119	1925	1933	Ex-Oldham, Ashton & Hyde; retrucked with Brill 21E
Middleton	27-34 batch	1903	1925	Oldham	120	1925	1935	Ex-Oldham, Ashton & Hyde; retrucked with Brill 21E
Newcastle	29	1901	1948	Grimsby & Immingham	6 (ii)	1948	1953	Rebuilt by Newcastle 1932/33
Newcastle	42	1901	1948	Grimsby & Immingham	7 (ii)	1948	1953	Rebuilt by Newcastle 1932/33
Newcastle	43	1901	1948	Gateshead	74	1948	1951	Rebuilt by Newcastle 1932/33
Newcastle	52	1901	1948	Gateshead	77	1948	1951	Rebuilt by Newcastle 1932/33
Newcastle	54	1901	1948	Gateshead	76	1948	1951	Rebuilt by Newcastle 1932/33
Newcastle	77	1901	1948	Grimsby & Immingham	8 (ii)	1948	1953	Rebuilt by Newcastle 1932/33
Newcastle	80	1901	1948	Gateshead	73	1948	1951	Rebuilt by Newcastle 1932/33
Newcastle	88	1901	1948	Gateshead	75	1948	1951	Rebuilt by Newcastle 1932/33

Original fleet	Original fleet number	Entered Service	Withdrawn	Second/third fleet	Second / third fleet number	Into service	Withdrawn	Notes
Newcastle	112	1901	1941	Sheffield	319	1941	1951	
Newcastle	113	1901	1941	Sheffield	313	1941	1951	
Newcastle	114	1901	1941	Sheffield	317	1941	1950	
Newcastle	116	1901	1941	Sheffield	318	1941	1951	
Newcastle	117	1901	1941	Sheffield	316	1941	1950	
Newcastle	118	1901	1941	Sheffield	315	1941	1951	
Newcastle	119	1901	1941	Sheffield	320	1941	1950	
Newcastle	122	1901	1941	Sheffield	311	1941	1951	
Newcastle	123	1901	1941	Sheffield	323	1941	1950	
Newcastle	124	1901	1941	Sheffield	312	1941	1950	
Newcastle	125	1901	1941	Sheffield	321	1941	1950	
Newcastle	126	1901	1941	Sheffield	322	1941	1950	
Newcastle	128	1901	1941	Sheffield	324	1941	1950	
Newcastle	129	1901	1941	Sheffield	314	1941	1950	
Norwich	One of 7, 9, 32 or 36	1899	1910	Coventry	37	1910	1940	Retrucked with Peckham P22 in 1916
Norwich	16	1899	1910	Coventry	38	1910	1940	Retrucked with Peckham P22 in 1916
Norwich	One of 7, 9, 32 or 36	1899	1910	Coventry	39	1910	1940	Retrucked with Peckham P22 in 1916
Norwich	One of 7, 9, 32 or 36	1899	1910	Coventry	40	1910	1940	Retrucked with Peckham P22 in 1916
Norwich	One of 7, 9, 32 or 36	1899	1910	Coventry	41	1910	1940	Retrucked with Peckham P22 in 1916
Nottingham	181-99 batch	1926	1936	Aberdeen	1 (ii)	1936	By 1951	
Nottingham	181-99 batch	1926	1936	Aberdeen	2 (ii)	1936	By 1951	
Nottingham	181-99 batch	1926	1936	Aberdeen	3 (ii)	1936	By 1951	
Nottingham	181-99 batch	1926	1936	Aberdeen	4 (ii)	1936	By 1951	
Nottingham	181-99 batch	1926	1936	Aberdeen	5 (ii)	1936	By 1951	
Nottingham	181-99 batch	1926	1936	Aberdeen	6 (ii)	1936	By 1951	
Nottingham	181-99 batch	1926	1936	Aberdeen	7 (ii)	1936	By 1951	
Nottingham	181-99 batch	1926	1936	Aberdeen	8 (ii)	1936	By 1951	
Nottingham	181-99 batch	1926	1936	Aberdeen	9 (ii)	1936	By 1951	

Location	Batch			Operator	No			Notes
Nottingham	181-99 batch	1926	1936	Aberdeen	10 (ii)	1936	By 1951	
Nottingham	181-99 batch	1926	1936	Aberdeen	11 (ii)	1936	By 1951	
Nottingham	181-99 batch	1926	1936	Aberdeen	12 (ii)	1936	By 1951	
Nottingham	181-99 batch	1926	1936	Aberdeen	13 (ii)	1936	By 1951	
Nottingham	181-99 batch	1926	1936	Aberdeen	14 (ii)	1936	By 1951	
Nottingham	181-99 batch	1926	1936	Aberdeen	15 (ii)	1936	By 1951	
Nottingham	181-99 batch	1926	1936	Aberdeen	16 (ii)	1936	By 1951	
Nottingham	181-99 batch	1926	1936	Aberdeen	17 (ii)	1936	By 1951	
Nottingham	181-99 batch	1926	1936	Aberdeen	18 (ii)	1936	1950	Used as works car following withdrawal
Nottingham	195	1926	1936	Aberdeen	Not allocated	1936	1936	Acquired for spares only
Notts & Derby	1-12 batch	1913	1925	Mansfield & District	29	1925	1926	Loaned
Notts & Derby	1-12 batch	1913	1925	Mansfield & District	30	1925	1932	
Notts & Derby	1-12 batch	1913	1925	Mansfield & District	31	1925	1932	
Notts & Derby	13-24 batch	1913	1929	Mansfield & District	29 (ii)	1929	1929	Loaned to replace No 26 damaged in an accident
Oldham	4, 5-12, 14-16 batch	1902	1916	Rotherham	38	1916	1919-29 era	Eight cars from batch sold to Walthamstow UDC in 1919; remaining three withdrawn 1929
Oldham	4, 5-12, 14-16 batch	1902	1916	Rotherham	39	1916	1919-29 era	Eight cars from batch sold to Walthamstow UDC in 1919; remaining three withdrawn 1929
Oldham	4, 5-12, 14-16 batch	1902	1916	Rotherham	40	1916	1919-29 era	Eight cars from batch sold to Walthamstow UDC in 1919; remaining three withdrawn 1929
Oldham	4, 5-12, 14-16 batch	1902	1916	Rotherham	41	1916	1919-29 era	Eight cars from batch sold to Walthamstow UDC in 1919; remaining three withdrawn 1929

Original fleet	Original fleet number	Entered Service	Withdrawn	Second/third fleet	Second / third fleet number	Into service	Withdrawn	Notes
Oldham	4, 5-12, 14-16 batch	1902	1916	Rotherham	42	1916	1919-29 era	Eight cars from batch sold to Walthamstow UDC in 1919; remaining three withdrawn 1929
Oldham	4, 5-12, 14-16 batch	1902	1916	Rotherham	43	1916	1919-29 era	Eight cars from batch sold to Walthamstow UDC in 1919; remaining three withdrawn 1929
Oldham	4, 5-12, 14-16 batch	1902	1916	Rotherham	44	1916	1918	Burnt out by fire
Oldham	4, 5-12, 14-16 batch	1902	1916	Rotherham	45	1916	1919-29 era	Eight cars from batch sold to Walthamstow UDC in 1919; remaining three withdrawn 1929
Oldham	4, 5-12, 14-16 batch	1902	1916	Rotherham	46	1916	1919-29 era	Eight cars from batch sold to Walthamstow UDC in 1919; remaining three withdrawn 1929
Oldham	4, 5-12, 14-16 batch	1902	1916	Rotherham	47	1916	1919-29 era	Eight cars from batch sold to Walthamstow UDC in 1919; remaining three withdrawn 1929
Oldham	4, 5-12, 14-16 batch	1902	1916	Rotherham	48	1916	1919-29 era	Eight cars from batch sold to Walthamstow UDC in 1919; remaining three withdrawn 1929
Oldham	4, 5-12, 14-16 batch	1902	1916	Rotherham	49	1916	1919-29 era	Eight cars from batch sold to Walthamstow UDC in 1919; remaining three withdrawn 1929

Oldham	17-26 batch	1902	1915	Great Grimsby	38	1915	1937	Passed to Cleethorpes UDC 1936
Oldham	17	1924	1946	Gateshead	35 (iii)	1946	1951	
Oldham	18	1924	1946	Gateshead	72	1946	1951	
Oldham	24	1924	1946	Gateshead	71	1946	1951	
Oldham	122	1926	1946	Gateshead	68	1946	1951	
Oldham	125	1926	1946	Gateshead	69	1946	1951	
Oldham	128	1926	1946	Gateshead	70	1946	1951	
Oldham, Ashton & Hyde / Manchester Corporation	1-18 batch	1899	1922	Ayr	25	1922	1931	
Oldham, Ashton & Hyde / Manchester Corporation	1-18 batch	1899	1922	Ayr	26	1922	1931	
Oldham, Ashton & Hyde / Manchester Corporation	1-18 batch	1899	1922	Ayr	27	1922	1931	
Oldham, Ashton & Hyde / Manchester Corporation	1-18 batch	1899	1922	Ayr	28	1922	1931	
Oldham, Ashton & Hyde	27-34 batch	1900	1903	Middleton	27	1903	1925	Passed to Oldham Corporation
Oldham, Ashton & Hyde	27-34 batch	1900	1903	Middleton	28	1903	1925	Passed to Oldham Corporation
Oldham, Ashton & Hyde	27-34 batch	1900	1903	Middleton	29	1903	1925	Passed to Oldham Corporation
Oldham, Ashton & Hyde	27-34 batch	1900	1903	Middleton	30	1903	1925	Passed to Oldham Corporation
Oldham, Ashton & Hyde	27-34 batch	1900	1903	Middleton	31	1903	1925	Passed to Oldham Corporation

Original fleet	Original fleet number	Entered Service	Withdrawn	Second/third fleet	Second / third fleet number	Into service	Withdrawn	Notes
Oldham, Ashton & Hyde	27-34 batch	1900	1903	Middleton	32	1903	1925	Passed to Oldham Corporation
Oldham, Ashton & Hyde	27-34 batch	1900	1903	Middleton	33	1903	1925	Passed to Oldham Corporation
Oldham, Ashton & Hyde	27-34 batch	1900	1903	Middleton	34	1903	1925	Passed to Oldham Corporation
Paisley District	53	1911	1914	Dundee	69	1914	1930	
Paisley District	54	1911	1914	Dundee	70	1914	1930	
Paisley District	55	1911	1914	Dundee	71	1914	1930	
Paisley District	56	1911	1914	Dundee	72	1914	1930	
Paisley District	57	1911	1914	Dundee	73	1914	1930	Renumbered 67 (ii) in 1927
Paisley District	58	1911	1914	Dundee	74	1914	1930	Renumbered 68 (ii) in 1927
Portsmouth	1	1930	1936	Sunderland	52 (ii)	1936	1953	
Potteries Electric Traction Co	71-85 batch	1900	c1915	Barrow-in-Furness	25	c1915		
Potteries Electric Traction Co	71-85 batch	1900	c1915	Barrow-in-Furness	26	c1915		
Potteries Electric Traction Co	82	1900	1928	Wemyss & District	20	1928	1932	
Potteries Electric Traction Co	95	1900/01	1928	Wemyss & District	21	1928	1932	
Preston	42	1929	1934	Lytham St Annes	56	1934		
Rawtenstall			1933	Darwen	9 (ii)	1933	1937	
Rawtenstall			1933	Darwen	10 (ii)	1933	1940	Top deck only
Rawtenstall			1933	Darwen	11 (ii)	1933	1937	
Rotherham	38-49 batch	1916	1919	Walthamstow	39	1919	1932	Ex-Oldham Corporation; new 1902.

Rotherham	38–49 batch	1916	1919	Walthamstow	1919	40	1932	Ex-Oldham Corporation; new 1902.
Rotherham	38–49 batch	1916	1919	Walthamstow	1919	41	1934	Ex-Oldham Corporation; new 1902. Renovated 1925 and renumbered in 47-50 batch
Rotherham	38–49 batch	1916	1919	Walthamstow	1919	42	1934	Ex-Oldham Corporation; new 1902. Renovated 1925 and renumbered in 47-50 batch
Rotherham	38–49 batch	1916	1919	Walthamstow	1919	43	1932	Ex-Oldham Corporation; new 1902.
Rotherham	38–49 batch	1916	1919	Walthamstow	1919	44	1934	Ex-Oldham Corporation; new 1902. Renovated 1925 and renumbered in 47-50 batch
Rotherham	38–49 batch	1916	1919	Walthamstow	1919	45	1934	Ex-Oldham Corporation; new 1902. Renovated 1925 and renumbered in 47-50 batch
Rotherham	38–49 batch	1916	1919	Walthamstow	1919	46	1932	Ex-Oldham Corporation; new 1902.
Rotherham	40 (ii)	1917	1926	Sheffield	1926	N/A	1926	Allocated Sheffield No 98 but not carried; LCC 'B' class; scrapped by Sheffield
Rotherham	41 (ii)	1917	1926	Sheffield	1926	96 (ii)	1931	LCC 'B' class
Rotherham	42 (ii)	1917	1926	Sheffield	1926	93 (ii)	1931	LCC 'B' class
Rotherham	43 (ii)	1917	1926	Sheffield	1926	91 (ii)	1931	LCC 'B' class
Rotherham	44 (ii)	1917	1926	Sheffield	1926	N/A	1926	Allocated Sheffield No 97 but not carried; LCC 'B' class; scrapped by Sheffield

Original fleet	Original fleet number	Entered Service	Withdrawn	Second/third fleet	Second / third fleet number	Into service	Withdrawn	Notes
Rotherham	45 (ii)	1917	1926	Sheffield	92 (ii)	1926	1931	LCC 'B' class
Rotherham	46 (ii)	1917	1926	Sheffield	94 (ii)	1926	1931	LCC 'B' class
Rotherham	47 (ii)	1917	1926	Sheffield	95 (ii)	1926	1931	LCC 'B' class
Rothesay	11-15 batch	1902	1915	Greenock & Port Glasgow	47 (?)	1915	By 1929	Re-equipped with replacement bogies
Rothesay	11-15 batch	1902	1915	Greenock & Port Glasgow	48 (?)	1915	By 1929	Re-equipped with replacement bogies
Sheerness & District	1-8 batch	1903	1917	Darlington	19	1918	1926	
Sheerness & District	1-8 batch	1903	1917	Darlington	20	1918	1926	
Sheerness & District	1-8 batch	1903	1917	Darlington	21	1918	1926	
Sheerness & District	1-8 batch	1903	1917	Darlington	22	1918	1926	
Sheerness & District	1-8 batch	1903	1917	Darlington	23	1918	1926	
Sheerness & District	1-8 batch	1903	1917	Darlington	24	1918	1926	
Sheerness & District	1-8 batch	1903	1917	Darlington	N/A	1918	1918	Acquired as source of spare parts
Sheerness & District	1-8 batch	1903	1917	Darlington	N/A	1918	1918	Acquired as source of spare parts
Sheerness & District	Unnumbered	1903	1903	City of Birmingham	189	1903	1912	See caption on page 46
Sheerness & District	Unnumbered	1903	1903	City of Birmingham	190	1903	1912	
Sheerness & District	Unnumbered	1903	1903	City of Birmingham	191	1903	1912	
Sheerness & District	Unnumbered	1903	1903	City of Birmingham	192	1903	1912	
Sheffield	56	1900	1918	Glossop	9	1918	1927	
Sheffield	202	1903	1920	Paisley	73 (?)	1920	1920	Did not enter service
Sheffield	Uncertain	1899/1900	1922	Gateshead	24 (ii)	1922	1951	
Sheffield	Uncertain	1899/1900	1922	Gateshead	25 (ii)	1922	1951	

Operator	No.	Built	Withdrawn	Disposal	Fleet No.	Year	Year	Notes
Sheffield	74	1900	1922	Gateshead	33 (ii)	1922	1951	Lower deck rescued for preservation and restored as Sheffield No 74
Sheffield	Uncertain	1899/1900	1922	Gateshead	36 (ii)	1922	1951	
Sheffield	40	1899	1920	Yorkshire (WD)	74-81 batch	1920	1951	
Sheffield	41	1899	1920	Barrow-in-Furness	29-34 batch	1920	1932	
Sheffield	43	1899	1920	Barrow-in-Furness	29-34 batch	1920	1932	
Sheffield	44	1899	1920	Yorkshire (WD)	74-81 batch	1920		
Sheffield	45	1899	1920	Yorkshire (WD)	74-81 batch	1920		
Sheffield	47	1899	1920	Yorkshire (WD)	74-81 batch	1920		
Sheffield	49	1899	1920	Yorkshire (WD)	74-81 batch	1920		
Sheffield	58	1899	1920	Potteries	121	1920		
Sheffield	Uncertain	1899/1900	1922	Gateshead	37 (ii)	1922	1951	
Sheffield	89	1900	1920	Preston	46-48 batch	1920	By 1935	No 48 renumbered 12 in 1929
Sheffield	90	1900	1920	Preston	46-48 batch	1920	By 1935	No 48 renumbered 12 in 1929
Sheffield	91	1900	1919	Yorkshire (WD)	70-73 batch	1919		
Sheffield	93	1900	1919	Yorkshire (WD)	70-73 batch	1919		
Sheffield	94	1900	1918	Musselburgh & District	17	1918		
Sheffield	95	1900	1920	Preston	46-48 batch	1920	By 1935	No 48 renumbered 12 in 1929
Sheffield	96 (or 97)	1899	1920	Potteries	122	1920	1922	
Sheffield	97 (or 96)	1899	1920	Potteries	123	1920		
Sheffield	100	1900	1920	Barrow-in-Furness	29-34 batch	1920	1932	
Sheffield	101	1900	1920	Yorkshire (WD)	74-81 batch	1920		

Original fleet	Original fleet number	Entered Service	Withdrawn	Second/third fleet	Second / third fleet number	Into service	Withdrawn	Notes
Sheffield	102	1900	1920	Barrow-in-Furness	29-34 batch	1920	1932	
Sheffield	103	1900	1919	Yorkshire (WD)	70-73 batch	1919		
Sheffield	125	1901	1918	Preston	40-45 batch	1918		
Sheffield	126	1901	1920	Barrow-in-Furness	29-34 batch	1920	1932	
Sheffield	128	1901	1920	Yorkshire (WD)	74-81 batch	1920		
Sheffield	129	1901	1918	Preston	40-45 batch	1918		
Sheffield	Uncertain	1902	1922	Gateshead	31 (ii)	1922	1951	
Sheffield	Uncertain	1902	1922	Gateshead	35 (ii)	1922	1947	
Sheffield	Uncertain	1902	1922	Gateshead	42 (ii)	1922	1951	
Sheffield	187	1902	1918	Preston	40-45 batch	1918		
Sheffield	188	1902	1918	Preston	40-45 batch	1918		
Sheffield	203	1903	1918	Musselburgh & District	18	1918	1928	
Sheffield	204	1903	1920	Yorkshire (WD)	74-81 batch	1920		
Sheffield	206	1902	1920	Barrow-in-Furness	29-34 batch	1920	1932	
Sheffield	207	1903	1918	Preston	40-45 batch	1918		
Sheffield	209	1903	1918	Preston	40-45 batch	1918		
Sheffield	210	1903	1918	Musselburgh & District	19	1918	1928	
Sheffield	211	1902	1919	Yorkshire (WD)	70-73 batch	1919		
Sheffield	141	1901	1923	Musselburgh & District	20	1923	1928	
Sheffield	170	1902	1923	Musselburgh & District	21	1923	1928	
Sheffield	252	1905	1923	Musselburgh & District	22	1923	1928	

South Lancashire Tramways	44	1927	1933	Bolton	33 (ii)	1933	By 1947	Renumbered 333 in 1940
South Lancashire Tramways	45	1927	1933	Bolton	34 (ii)	1933	By 1947	Renumbered 334 in 1940
South Lancashire Tramways	47	1901/02	1933	Bolton	35 (ii)	1933	By 1947	Rebuilt 1923-25; renumbered 335 in 1940
South Lancashire Tramways	48	1901/02	1933	Bolton	36 (ii)	1933	By 1947	Rebuilt 1923-25; renumbered 336 in 1940
South Lancashire Tramways	50	1901/02	1933	Bolton	37 (ii)	1933	By 1947	Rebuilt 1923-25; renumbered 337 in 1940
South Lancashire Tramways	54	1901/02	1933	Bolton	38 (ii)	1933	By 1947	Rebuilt 1923-25; renumbered 338 in 1940
South Lancashire Tramways	55	1901/02	1933	Bolton	39 (ii)	1933	By 1947	Rebuilt 1923-25; renumbered 339 in 1940
South Lancashire Tramways	58	1901/02	1933	Bolton	40 (ii)	1933	By 1947	Rebuilt 1923-25; renumbered 340 in 1940
South Shields	52 (ii)	1936	1946	Sunderland	48	1946	1954	
Southampton	7	1925	1949	Leeds	N/A	Never	Never	Ex-No 1; scrapped in Southampton
Southampton	8	1925	1949	Leeds	N/A	Never	Never	Ex-No 5; scrapped in Southampton
Southampton	10	1925	1949	Leeds	(306 [ii])	Never	1951	Ex-No 2
Southampton	12	1923	1949	Leeds	N/A	Never	Never	Scrapped in Southampton
Southampton	14	1924	1949	Leeds	N/A	Never	1950	Scrapped in Farsley
Southampton	16	1924	1949	Leeds	N/A	Never	Never	Scrapped in Southampton
Southampton	17	1924	1949	Leeds	N/A	Never	Never	Ex-No 1; scrapped in Southampton
Southampton	18	1924	1949	Leeds	(305 [ii])	Never	1951	

Original fleet	Original fleet number	Entered Service	Withdrawn	Second/third fleet	Second / third fleet number	Into service	Withdrawn	Notes
Southampton	19	1924	1949	Leeds	(311 [i])	Never	1951	
Southampton	20	1925	1949	Leeds	N/A	Never	Never	Ex-No 1; scrapped in Southampton
Southampton	21	1931	1949	Leeds	N/A	Never	1950	Scrapped in Farsley
Southampton	22	1928	1949	Leeds	N/A	Never	1950	Scrapped in Farsley
Southampton	23	1930	1949	Leeds	300 (ii)	1950	1953	
Southampton	25	1930	1949	Leeds	299 (ii)	1951	1953	
Southampton	32	1930	1949	Leeds	298 (ii)	1950	1952	
Southampton	35	1930	1949	Leeds	297 (ii)	1950	1953	
Southampton	37	1929	1949	Leeds	N/A	Never	1950	Scrapped in Farsley
Southampton	50	1930	1949	Leeds	296 (ii)	1950	1952	
Southampton	74	1929	1949	Leeds	N/A	Never	Never	Scrapped in Southampton
Southampton	92	1926	1949	Leeds	(304 [ii])	Never	1951	
Southampton	93	1926	1949	Leeds	N/A	Never	Never	Scrapped in Southampton
Southampton	94	1926	1949	Leeds	N/A	Never	Never	Scrapped in Southampton
Southampton	95	1927	1949	Leeds	(304 [ii])	Never	1951	
Southampton	96	1927	1949	Leeds	N/A	Never	1950	Scrapped in Farsley
Southampton	97	1927	1949	Leeds	(307 [ii])	Never	1951	
Southampton	98	1927	1949	Leeds	N/A	Never	1950	Scrapped in Farsley
Southampton	99	1927	1949	Leeds	(303 [ii])	Never	1951	
Southampton	100	1928	1949	Leeds	(312 [ii])	Never	1951	
Southampton	101	1928	1949	Leeds	(310 [ii])	Never	1951	
Southampton	102	1929	1949	Leeds	(308 [ii])	Never	1951	
Southampton	103	1929	1949	Leeds	(301 [ii])	Never	1951	
Southampton	104	1929	1949	Leeds	295 (ii)	1950	1952	
Southampton	105	1930	1949	Leeds	294 (ii)	1949	1953	
Southampton	106	1930	1949	Leeds	293 (ii)	1949	1952	
Southampton	107	1930	1949	Leeds	292 (ii)	1949	1952	
Southampton	108	1930	1949	Leeds	290 (ii)	1949	1953	
Southampton	109	1930	1949	Leeds	291 (ii)	1949	1952	
Southport	1-11 batch	1900	1920	Barrow-in-Furness	1 (ii)	1920	1930	

Operator	Batch				Number			Notes
Southport	1-11 batch	1900	1920	Barrow-in-Furness	2 (ii)	1920	1930	Converted into works car
Southport	1-11 batch	1900	1920	Barrow-in-Furness	3 (ii)	1920	1930	Converted into works car
Southport	1-11 batch	1900	1920	Barrow-in-Furness	4 (ii)	1920	1930	
Sunderland	85	1931	1944	Leeds	288 (ii)	1944	1957	Converted into No 600 in 1953. Preserved on withdrawal; now based at NTM
Sunderland District	1920 batch	1920	1924	Bolton	131	1924	1933	The batch was numbered 35-38 by Sunderland & District plus four others that replaced older cars; numbers unknown.
Sunderland District	1920 batch	1920	1924	Bolton	132	1924	1933	
Sunderland District	1920 batch	1920	1924	Bolton	133	1924	1933	
Sunderland District	1920 batch	1920	1924	Bolton	134	1924	1933	
Sunderland District	1920 batch	1920	1924	Bolton	135	1924	1933	
Sunderland District	1920 batch	1920	1924	Bolton	136	1924	1933	
Sunderland District	1920 batch	1920	1924	Bolton	137	1924	1933	
Sunderland District	1920 batch	1920	1924	Bolton	138	1924	1933	
Sunderland District	8 (ii), 16-30 batch	1913	1925	Grimsby	41	1925	1937	
Sunderland District	8 (ii), 16-30 batch	1913	1925	Grimsby	42	1925	1937	
Sunderland District	8 (ii), 16-30 batch	1913	1925	Grimsby	43	1925	1937	
Sunderland District	8 (ii), 16-30 batch	1913	1925	Grimsby	44	1925	1937	
Sunderland District	8 (ii), 16-30 batch	1913	1925	Grimsby	45	1925	1937	

Original fleet	Original fleet number	Entered Service	Withdrawn	Second/third fleet	Second / third fleet number	Into service	Withdrawn	Notes
Sunderland District	8 (ii), 16-30 batch	1913	1925	Grimsby	46	1925	1937	
Sunderland District	8 (ii), 16-30 batch	1913	1925	Grimsby	47	1925	1937	
Sunderland District	8 (ii), 16-30 batch	1913	1925	Grimsby	48	1925	1937	
Sunderland District	8 (ii), 16-30 batch	1913	1925	Grimsby	49	1925	1937	
Sunderland District	8 (ii), 16-30 batch	1913	1925	Grimsby	50	1925	1937	
Sunderland District	8 (ii), 16-30 batch	1913	1925	Grimsby	51	1925	1937	
Sunderland District	8 (ii), 16-30 batch	1913	1925	Grimsby	52	1925	1937	
Sunderland District	8 (ii), 16-30 batch	1913	1925	Grimsby	53	1925	1937	
Sunderland District	8 (ii), 16-30 batch	1913	1925	Grimsby	54	1925	1937	
Sunderland District	8 (ii), 16-30 batch	1913	1925	Grimsby	55	1925	1937	
Sunderland District	8 (ii), 16-30 batch	1913	1925	Grimsby	56	1925	1937	
Taunton	1 -6 batch	1901	1905	Leamington & Warwick	7	1905	1930	
Taunton	1 -6 batch	1901	1905	Leamington & Warwick	8	1905	1930	
Taunton	1 -6 batch	1901	1905	Leamington & Warwick	9	1905	1930	
Taunton	1 -6 batch	1901	1905	Leamington & Warwick	10	1905	1930	
Taunton	1 -6 batch	1901	1905	Leamington & Warwick	11	1905	1930	
Taunton	1 -6 batch	1902	1905	Leamington & Warwick	12	1905	1930	
Taunton	1-6 (ii) batch	1905	1921	Gravesend & Northfleet	7 (ii)	1921	1929	Converted into one-man car
Taunton	1-6 (ii) batch	1905	1921	Gravesend & Northfleet	8 (ii)	1921	1929	
Taunton	1-6 (ii) batch	1905	1921	Torquay	34	1921	1934	Modified for one-man operation
Taunton	1-6 (ii) batch	1905	1921	Torquay	35	1921	1934	Modified for one-man operation

Taunton	1-6 (ii) batch	1905	1921	Torquay	36	1921	1934	Modified for one-man operation
Torquay	7	1906	1934	Plymouth	16 (ii)	1934	By 1936	
Torquay	9	1906	1934	Plymouth	17 (ii)	1934	By 1936	
Torquay	10	1906	1934	Plymouth	18 (ii)	1934	By 1936	
Torquay	16	1906	1934	Plymouth	19 (ii)	1934	By 1936	
Torquay	17	1906	1934	Plymouth	20 (ii)	1934	By 1936	
Torquay	18	1906	1934	Plymouth	21 (ii)	1934	By 1936	
Torquay	37	1923	1934	Plymouth	12 (ii)	1934	1938	Scrapped 1942
Torquay	38	1923	1934	Plymouth	13 (ii)	1934	1938	Scrapped 1942
Torquay	39	1925	1934	Plymouth	14 (ii)	1934	1938	Scrapped 1942
Torquay	40	1925	1934	Plymouth	15 (ii)	1934	1938	Scrapped 1942
Torquay	41	1925	1934	Plymouth	10(ii)	1934	1938	Scrapped 1942
Torquay	42	1925	1934	Plymouth	11 (ii)	1934	1938	Scrapped 1942
Tyneside Tramways	3	1902	1930	South Shields	46	1930	1936/37	Cut down to single-deck in 1933
Tyneside Tramways	4	1902	1930	South Shields	47	1930	1937/38	
Wemyss & District	18	1925		Dunfermline & District	45 (ii)	1932	1937	
Wemyss & District	19	1925		Dunfermline & District	44 (ii)	1932	1937	
West Hartlepool	1 (ii)	1914	1927	Dover	1 (ii)	1 (ii)	1936	
West Hartlepool	2 (ii)	1914	1927	Dover	2 (ii)	2 (ii)	1936	
West Hartlepool	3 (ii)	1914	1927	Dover	3 (ii)	3 (ii)	1936	
West Hartlepool	4 (ii)	1914	1927	Dover	4 (ii)	4 (ii)	1936	
West Hartlepool	5 (ii)	1914	1927	Dover	5 (ii)	5 (ii)	1936	
Weston-super-Mare	1-12 batch	1902	1904	Swansea	46	1904	1937	Rebuilt 1922
Weston-super-Mare	1-12 batch	1902	1904	Swansea	47	1904	1937	Rebuilt 1922
Weston-super-Mare	1-12 batch	1902	1904	Swansea	48	1904	1937	Rebuilt 1922

Original fleet	Original fleet number	Entered Service	Withdrawn	Second/third fleet	Second / third fleet number	Into service	Withdrawn	Notes
Weston-super-Mare	1-12 batch	1902	1904	Swansea	49	1904	1937	Rebuilt 1922
Wigan	1 -12 batch	1900	1904	Coventry	19 (ii)	1904	1940	Rebuilt 1930
Wigan	1 -12 batch	1900	1904	Coventry	20 (ii)	1904	1934	
Wigan	1 -12 batch	1900	1904	Coventry	21	1904	1934	
Wigan	1 -12 batch	1900	1904	Coventry	22	1904	1940	
Wigan	1 -12 batch	1900	1904	Coventry	23	1904	1940	
Wigan	1 -12 batch	1900	1904	Coventry	24	1904	1930	
Wigan	1 -12 batch	1900	1904	Coventry	25	1904	1934	
Wigan	1 -12 batch	1900	1904	Coventry	26	1904	1940	
Wigan	1 -12 batch	1900	1904	Coventry	27	1904	1940	Converted into a snowplough 1930
Wigan	1 -12 batch	1900	1904	Coventry	28	1904	1940	
Wigan	1 -12 batch	1900	1904	Coventry	29	1904	1934	
Wigan	1 -12 batch	1900	1904	Coventry	30	1904	1940	Converted into a snowplough 1930
Wigan	1 (ii)	1914	1931	South Shields	51	1932	1945	Rebuilt as fully enclosed before re-entering service
Wigan	2 (ii)	1914	1931	South Shields	52	1932	1945	Rebuilt as fully enclosed before re-entering service; renumbered 33 (ii) in 1935
Wigan	3 (ii)	1914	1931	South Shields	N/A	1932	1934	Purchased but never used
Wigan	4 (ii)	1914	1931	South Shields	23 (ii)	1932	1945	Rebuilt as fully enclosed before re-entering service
Wigan	5 (ii)	1914	1931	South Shields	N/A	1932	1934	Purchased but never used
Wigan	6 (ii)	1914	1931	South Shields	50	1932	1945	Rebuilt as fully enclosed before re-entering service
Wigan	68 or 77	1904/05	1927	St Helens	30 (ii)	1927	1935	Renumbered 13 (ii) 1929

Wigan	68 or 77	1904/05	1927	St Helens	31 (ii)	1927	1935	Renumbered 14 (ii) 1929
Worcester	16	1921	1928	Cheltenham & District	25	1928	1930	
Worcester	17	1921	1928	Cheltenham & District	24	1928	1930	
Yorkshire (West Riding)	1920 batch of eight cars	1920	1932	South Shields	18 (ii)	1932	By 1939	Were Nos 28, 31, 34, 35 and 37 plus three others in the Yorkshire (WR) fleet
Yorkshire (West Riding)	1920 batch of eight cars	1920	1932	South Shields	20 (ii)	1932	By 1939	Were Nos 28, 31, 34, 35 and 37 plus three others in the Yorkshire (WR) fleet
Yorkshire (Woollen District)	19	1902/03	1903	Barnsley & District	19	1903	1904	Hired from Yorkshire and retained original fleet number
Yorkshire (Woollen District)	20	1902/03	1903	Barnsley & District	20	1903	1904	Hired from Yorkshire and retained original fleet number
Yorkshire (Woollen District)	29	1902/03	1903	Barnsley & District	29	1903	1904	Hired from Yorkshire and retained original fleet number
Yorkshire (Woollen District)	59	1904	1905	Barnsley & District	13	1905	By 1930	

Notes:

Numbers in brackets were allocated but never carried.

'N/A' indicates that no new number was allocated.

'Batch' indicates that the available records do not permit the exact correlation of old and new fleet numbers.

BIBLIOGRAPHY

Anderson, R.C.: *The Tramways of East Anglia*: LRTL; 1969

Bett, W.H., and Gillham, J.C, edited by Price, J.H.; *The Tramways of Eastern Scotland*; LRTA; undated

Bett, W.H., and Gillham, J.C, edited by Price, J.H.; *The Tramways of North Lancashire*; LRTA; undated

Bett, W.H., and Gillham, J.C, edited by Price, J.H.; *The Tramways of North-East England*; LRTL; undated

Bett, W.H., and Gillham, J.C, edited by Price, J.H.; *The Tramways of South Wales*; LRTA; undated

Bett, W.H., and Gillham, J.C, edited by Price, J.H.; *The Tramways of South West England*; LRTA; undated

Bett, W.H., and Gillham, J.C, edited by Price, J.H.; *The Tramways of South-East Lancashire*; LRTL; undated

Bett, W.H., and Gillham, J.C, edited by Price, J.H.; *The Tramways of the East Midlands*; LRTL; undated

Bett, W.H., and Gillham, J.C, edited by Price, J.H.; *The Tramways of the East Midlands*; LRTL; undated

Bett, W.H., and Gillham, J.C, edited by Price, J.H.; *The Tramways of the South Midlands*; LRTA; undated

Bett, W.H., and Gillham, J.C, edited by Price, J.H.; *The Tramways of Yorkshire and Humberside*; LRTA; undated

Bett, W.H., and Gillham, J.C, edited by Wiseman, R.J.S.; *The Tramways of the West Midlands*; LRTA; undated

Brook, Roy; *Huddersfield Corporation Tramways*; Author; 1983

Brotchie, A.W. and, Grieves, R.L.; *Dumbarton's Trams and Buses*; NB Traction; 1985

Brotchie, A.W., and Grieves, R.L.; *Dumbarton's Trams and Buses*; NB Traction; 1985

Brotchie, Alan W.; *Scottish Tramway Fleets*; NB Traction; 1968

Brotchie, Alan; *Tramways of Fife and the Forth Valley – Part 3: The Wemyss and District Tramways Co Ltd*; NB Traction; 1976

Burrows, V.E.; *The Tramways of Southend-on-Sea*; Advertiser Press; 1965

Cormack, Ian. L.; *The Rothesay Tramways Company 1879-1949 STTS*; 1986

G.E. Baddeley edited by J.H. Price; *The Tramways of Kent*; LRTA; undated

Gandy, Kenneth; *Sheffield Corporation Tramways*; Sheffield City Libraries; 1985

Gentry, P.W.; *The Tramways of the West of England*; 1952; Published by the author and C.S.N. Walker; 1952

Gillham, J.C. and Wiseman, R.J.S.; *The Tramways of South Lancashire and North Wales*; LRTA; undated

Gillham, J.C. and Wiseman, R.J.S.; *The Tramways of the South Coast*; LRTA; undated

Gillham, J.C. and Wiseman, R.J.S.; *The Tramways of West Yorkshire*; LRTA; undated

Gillham, J.C. and Wiseman, R.J.S.; *The Tramways of Western Scotland*; LRTA; undated

Hearse, George S.; *The Tramways of Jarrow and South Shields*; Published by the author; 1971

Hearse, George S.; *The Tramways of Northumberland*; Published by the author; 1961

Hesketh, Peter; *Trams in the North West*; Ian Allan Ltd; 1995

Horn, J.V.; *Dover Corporation Tramways 1897-1936*; LRTL; 1955

Hunter, D.L.G.; *Edinburgh's Transport*; Advertise Press; 1964

Hurst, Tony; *Mansfield's Trams*; Irwell Press; 2002

Hyde, W.G.S.; *A History of Public Transport in Ashton-under-Lyne*; MTMS; 1980

Invicta; *The Tramways of Kent – Volume 2*; LRTL/TLRS; 1975

Johnson, Ian; *The Pilcher Pullman Cars Built 1930-1932*; MTMS; 2010

King, J.S.; *Bradford Corporation Tramways*; Venture; 1998

Maggs, Colin; *Newport Trams*; Oakwood Press; 1977

Oakley, E.R.; *London County Council Tramways – Volume 1: South London*; LTHG; 1989

Palmer, Steve, and Turner, Brian; *Blackpool by Tram* (Third Edition); Published by the authors; 1981

Pickles, W.; *The Tramways of Dewsbury & Wakefield*; LRTL; 1980

Rodinglea; *The Tramways of East London*; TLRS/LRTL; 1967

Sambourne, R. C.; *Plymouth – 100 Years of Street Travel*; Glasney Press; 1972

Smeeton, C.S.; *The London United Tramways: Volume 1 – Origins to 1912*; LRTA/TLRS; 1994

Soper, J.; *Leeds Transport – Volume 3: 1932-1953*; LTHS; 2003

Southeastern; *The Tramways of Woolwich and South East London*; LRTL/TLRS; 1963

Staddon, S.A.; *The Tramways of Sunderland*; Advertiser Press; 1964

Stewart, Ian; *The Glasgow Tramcar*; STMS; 1983

Swingle, S.L, and Turner, K.; *The Leamington & Warwick Tramways*; Oakwood Press; 1970

Taylor, C.; *Manchester's Transport – Part 1: Tramway & Trolleybus Rolling Stock*; Manchester Transport Historical Collection; 1965

Thornton, Eric, and King, Stanley; *Halifax Corporation Tramways*; LRTA; 2005

Turner, Keith; *The Llandudno & Colwyn Bay Electric Railway*; Oakwood Press; 1993

Waller, Michael H., and Waller, Peter; *British & Irish Tramway Systems since 1945*; Ian Allan Publishing; 1992

Waller, Peter; *Regional Tramways: London*; Pen & Sword; 2019

Waller, Peter; *Regional Tramways: Scotland*; Pen & Sword; 2016

Waller, Peter; *Regional Tramways: The North-West England post 1945*; Pen & Sword; 2017

Waller, Peter; *Regional Tramways: Wales, Isle of Man & Ireland post 1945*; Pen & Sword; 2017

Waller, Peter; *Regional Tramways: Yorkshire & North East of England*; Pen & Sword; 2016

Waller, Peter; *Regional Tramways: Yorkshire & North East of England*; Pen & Sword; 2016

Waller, Peter; *The Classic Trams*; Ian Allan Ltd; 1993

Willoughby, D.W., and Oakley, E.R.; *London Transport Tramways Handbook*; Published by the authors; 1972